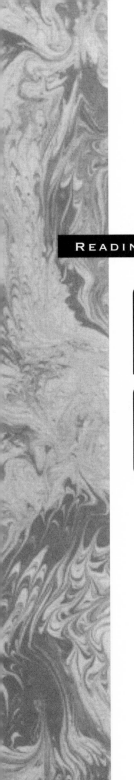

READINGS ON

A CHRISTMAS CAROL

OTHER TITLES IN THE GREENHAVEN PRESS LITERARY COMPANION SERIES:

BRITISH AUTHORS

Jane Austen
Joseph Conrad
Charles Dickens
J.R.R. Tolkien

BRITISH LITERATURE

Animal Farm
Beowulf
Brave New World
The Canterbury Tales
Frankenstein
Great Expectations
Gulliver's Travels
Hamlet
Heart of Darkness
Jane Eyre
Julius Caesar

Lord of the Flies
Macbeth
The Merchant of Venice
Othello
A Portrait of the Artist
  as a Young Man
Pride and Prejudice
Romeo and Juliet
Shakespeare: The Comedies
Shakespeare: The Histories
Shakespeare: The Sonnets
Shakespeare: The Tragedies
Silas Marner
A Tale of Two Cities
The Taming of the Shrew
Tess of the d'Urbervilles
Wuthering Heights

ᴾRESS

anion

TO BRITISH LITERATURE

READINGS ON

A CHRISTMAS CAROL

Jill Karson, *Book Editor*

David L. Bender, *Publisher*

Bruno Leone, *Executive Editor*

Bonnie Szumski, *Series Editor*

Every effort has been made to trace the owners of copyrighted material. The articles in this volume may have been edited for content, length, and/or reading level. The titles have been changed to enhance the editorial purpose. Those interested in locating the original source will find the complete citation on the first page of each article.

Library of Congress Cataloging-in-Publication Data

Readings on A Christmas carol / Jill Karson, book editor.
     p.   cm. — (The Greenhaven Press literary
companion to British literature)
Includes bibliographical references and index.
ISBN 0-7377-0340-7 — ISBN 0-7377-0339-3 (pbk.)
     1. Dickens, Charles, 1812–1870. Christmas carol.
     2. Christmas stories, English—History and criticism.
I. Karson, Jill. II. Series.

PR4572.C7 R43   2000
—dc21   99-047966

Copyright ©2000 by Greenhaven Press, Inc.
PO Box 289009
San Diego, CA 92198-9009
Printed in the U.S.A.

> *I have endeavoured in this Ghostly little book, to raise the Ghost of an Idea, which shall not put my readers out of humour with themselves, with each other, with the season, or with me. May it haunt their house pleasantly.*

Charles Dickens

CONTENTS

Chapter 1: Design and Imagery in *A Christmas Carol*

1. The Function of Time *by Robert L. Patten*   38
The *Carol* takes place within twenty-four hours in Scrooge's life, yet his conversion is contingent upon a multiplicity of time, including past times, a fictive present, and a potential future.

2. *A Christmas Carol*'s Fairy-Tale Format *by Harry Stone*   45
Dickens perfectly melds a fairy-tale atmosphere that allows him to commingle realistic detail with magical happenings. This structure enables Dickens to use extraordinary events to convey the story's moral lesson.

3. The Character of the Narrator *by James A. Davies*   55
In *A Christmas Carol*, the narrator, described as patronizing and emotionally withdrawn, exerts a powerful influence in the telling of events.

Chapter 2: Themes in *A Christmas Carol*

1. *A Christmas Carol* and the Search for Lost Innocence *by Elliot L. Gilbert*   68
A Christmas Carol is the metaphysical study of Scrooge's rediscovery of his own innocence. Only when he reestablishes his metaphysical innocence can he open his heart and stop hoarding material goods.

2. *A Christmas Carol* and the Economic Man *by Edgar Johnson*   83
Scrooge exemplifies a callous economic philosophy based on the perpetuation of money and power. Scrooge's conversion is emblematic of the change of heart Dickens hopes all mankind will experience.

Chapter 3: *A Christmas Carol:* Dickens's Christmas Vision

Chapter 4: Biblical Allusions in *A Christmas Carol*

FOREWORD

> *"'Tis the good reader that*
> *makes the good book."*
>
> Ralph Waldo Emerson

The story's bare facts are simple: The captain, an old and scarred seafarer, walks with a peg leg made of whale ivory. He relentlessly drives his crew to hunt the world's oceans for the great white whale that crippled him. After a long search, the ship encounters the whale and a fierce battle ensues. Finally the captain drives his harpoon into the whale, but the harpoon line catches the captain about the neck and drags him to his death.

A simple story, a straightforward plot—yet, since the 1851 publication of Herman Melville's *Moby-Dick*, readers and critics have found many meanings in the struggle between Captain Ahab and the whale. To some, the novel is a cautionary tale that depicts how Ahab's obsession with revenge leads to his insanity and death. Others believe that the whale represents the unknowable secrets of the universe and that Ahab is a tragic hero who dares to challenge fate by attempting to discover this knowledge. Perhaps Melville intended Ahab as a criticism of Americans' tendency to become involved in well-intentioned but irrational causes. Or did Melville model Ahab after himself, letting his fictional character express his anger at what he perceived as a cruel and distant god?

Although literary critics disagree over the meaning of *Moby-Dick*, readers do not need to choose one particular interpretation in order to gain an understanding of Melville's novel. Instead, by examining various analyses, they can gain numerous insights into the issues that lie under the surface of the basic plot. Studying the writings of literary critics can also aid readers in making their own assessments of *Moby-Dick* and other literary works and in developing analytical thinking skills.

The Greenhaven Literary Companion Series was created with these goals in mind. Designed for young adults, this unique anthology series provides an engaging and comprehensive introduction to literary analysis and criticism. The essays included in the Literary Companion Series are chosen for their accessibility to a young adult audience and are expertly edited in consideration of both the reading and comprehension levels of this audience. In addition, each essay is introduced by a concise summation that presents the contributing writer's main themes and insights. Every anthology in the Literary Companion Series contains a varied selection of critical essays that cover a wide time span and express diverse views. Wherever possible, primary sources are represented through excerpts from authors' notebooks, letters, and journals and through contemporary criticism.

Each title in the Literary Companion Series pays careful consideration to the historical context of the particular author or literary work. In-depth biographies and detailed chronologies reveal important aspects of authors' lives and emphasize the historical events and social milieu that influenced their writings. To facilitate further research, every anthology includes primary and secondary source bibliographies of articles and/or books selected for their suitability for young adults. These engaging features make the Greenhaven Literary Companion series ideal for introducing students to literary analysis in the classroom or as a library resource for young adults researching the world's great authors and literature.

Exceptional in its focus on young adults, the Greenhaven Literary Companion Series strives to present literary criticism in a compelling and accessible format. Every title in the series is intended to spark readers' interest in leading American and world authors, to help them broaden their understanding of literature, and to encourage them to formulate their own analyses of the literary works that they read. It is the editors' hope that young adult readers will find these anthologies to be true companions in their study of literature.

INTRODUCTION

It has been over 150 years since Scrooge first uttered the now famous words, "Bah! Humbug!" Yet *A Christmas Carol's* appeal has not faded with time. Like Dickens's contemporaries, modern readers ritualistically read the book or see its play adaptation every Christmas, enjoying the familiar ghoulish spirits, snowy, fog-bound streets, blazing hearths, and, of course, the "squeezing, wrenching, grasping, scraping, clutching, covetous, old sinner" Scrooge. No wonder many readers can recite particular scenes by heart—miserly Scrooge's quips, for example, or Tiny Tim's musings.

The Carol, though, is much more than a collection of memorable scenes. English novelist William Thackeray once called the Carol "a national benefit, and to every man and woman who reads it a personal kindness." Indeed, that such an unregenerate miscreant as Scrooge can open his heart to his fellow man is quintessential Dickens, the finest expression of his love of—and hope for—humanity.

Readings on A Christmas Carol is designed to offer readers a number of critical views on this enduring story. This book includes essays from a variety of sources. Several identify major themes in the *Carol;* others discuss Dickens's purpose and design, how the author melds his story to carry his message. Each essay begins with a brief introduction that highlights the authors' main ideas. A biography and chronology describe significant events in Dickens's life and places them in a broader historical context. Other research aids include a synopsis of plot and list of characters, a detailed bibliography and an annotated table of contents. Together, these features make this volume an indispensable tool to readers studying, as Dickens critic Edward Newton once called, "the greatest little book in the world."

CHARLES DICKENS: A BIOGRAPHY

Charles Dickens exuded an energy and determination that awed friends and overwhelmed relatives. His temper flared at slights to himself and his work; his generosity and compassion extended to children and the working poor. He was a pessimist who doubted that government and the upper class would ever pass reforms to help poor people, but who optimistically believed in the goodness of the lower class and championed their cause throughout his life. He made his mark in nineteenth-century England with humor, creating a cast of characters that exemplified all that he loved and satirized all that he hated about his society. Biographer Edgar Johnson says in the preface to his biography of Dickens:

> Dickens was himself a Dickens character, bursting with an inordinate and fantastic vitality. The world in which his spirit dwelt was identical with the world of his novels, brilliant in hue, violent in movement, crammed with people all furiously alive and with places as alive as his people. "The Dickens world" was his everyday world.

Scholars attribute much of the formation of Dickens's personality and, consequently, his achievements to two phases in his boyhood years. The first, happy phase gave him hope and optimism; the second, sad phase instilled his spirit for social reform.

Charles John Huffman Dickens was born on February 7, 1812, in the southwestern English town of Landport in Portsea, the second of eight children born to John and Elizabeth Barrow Dickens. John Dickens, a clerk in the Navy Payoffice, and Elizabeth, a pretty, educated woman, belonged to the middle class, but were not prosperous enough to withstand the extravagant spending and entertainment they enjoyed. John Dickens enjoyed a house full of party guests and rehearsed little Charles and his sister to entertain them. In *Charles Dickens: A Critical Study,* G.K. Chesterton says:

> Some of the earliest glimpses we have of Charles Dickens show him to us perched on some chair or table singing comic songs in an atmosphere of perpetual applause. So, almost as soon as he can toddle, he steps into the glare of the footlights. He never stepped out of it until he died.

In 1814 John was temporarily sent to the London office before being transferred to the naval dockyards in the southeastern town of Chatham in 1817, when Charles was five.

There John rented a large house for his family, two servants, and Aunt Fanny, his wife's widowed sister, but soon found it beyond his means and moved his family to a smaller Chatham home.

A HAPPY AND SAD CHILDHOOD

In a family that felt financially secure, Charles enjoyed his years in Chatham, five years that permanently affected his outlook on life. He played games with friends, put on magic-lantern shows (an early form of slide projector), and continued to sing duets with his sister Fanny. Mary Weller, the maid who cared for the children, told bedtime stories and hummed evensong, or evening worship, hymns. Dickens investigated the town, recording in his mind the sights of its shipwrights, convict laborers, guild hall, cathedral, and castle on the hill and the smells of rope and wood and canvas down by the docks. Because he was often sick, Charles never played sports well, but he loved to read, saying later, "When I think of it, the picture always arises in my mind of a summer evening, the boys at play in the churchyard, and I sitting on my bed, reading as if for life." In addition to reading the family books, such as *Peregrine Pickle, Don Quixote,* and *Robinson Crusoe,* Aunt Fanny's suitor, Dr. Matthew Lamert, and his son James took Charles to farces, melodramas, and to *Richard II* and *Macbeth.*

Dickens attended the school of William Giles, a Baptist minister in Chatham. A precocious child, Charles fully expected to attend both school and college and enter a profession. These early happy years laid the groundwork for his lifelong hope and vitality.

His hopes for a bright future were dashed, however, when his father, now heavily in debt, was transferred back to London in 1822, when Charles was ten. John Dickens settled his family in Camden Town, a poor section of London, in a four-room house that held Dickens's parents as well as six children, one maid, and James Lamert, who lived with them. No arrangement was made for Charles to go to school, though Fanny had won a scholarship to the Royal Academy of Music. Charles did chores at home, and just as curiously as he had done in Chatham, he wandered the streets of Camden Town, observing its noisy vehicles, small factories, taverns, cooked-food stalls, and rubbish dumps and watching chimney sweeps, muffin-boys, and apprentices at work—all sounds, sights, and smells that imprinted themselves on his mind.

Not long after moving to London, Charles learned what it meant to be poor. One sad day his family sold his beloved books from Chatham days to pay debts, after which he borrowed copies of the newspapers *Spectator* and *Tatler* for his reading. His mother rented a room and started a school, but not one pupil came. James Lamert, who managed a boot-blacking factory, suggested that Charles work there to help with the deteriorating family finances. At twelve, Charles worked from eight A.M. to eight P.M. for six shillings a week in the tumbledown warehouse tying and labeling pots of blacking. Two weeks after Charles started at the blacking factory, John Dickens was arrested for not paying his debts and sent to Marshalsea, a debtors prison, or workhouse for the poor, with meager food and hard labor. Charles was sent out to pawn household goods, and when only beds, chairs, and the kitchen table were left, the rest of the family moved to Marshalsea (which admitted groups in family quarters) with the father.

John Dickens, who still drew a small naval salary, paid for lodgings so that Charles could continue his job at the blacking factory. Now that he had to feed himself on six shillings a week, he divided his money into packages, one for each day, occasionally splurging the whole day's allotment on a sweet or a good ale; when he had no money, he walked to the Covent Garden market and stared at food. Alone in the lodging house with no companion but the boys from the blacking factory, who mocked him because he was small and shy and different, Charles suffered greatly. In an unpublished autobiography, he later wrote of this time in his life:

> No words can express the secret agony of my soul, as I sunk into this companionship; compared these everyday associates with those of my happier childhood; and felt my early hopes of growing up to be a learned and distinguished man, crushed in my breast.

> The deep remembrance of the sense I had of being utterly neglected and hopeless; of the shame I felt in my position; of the misery it was to my young heart to believe that, day by day, what I had learned, and thought, and delighted in, and raised my fancy and my emulation up by, was passing away from me, never to be brought back any more; . . . even now, famous and caressed and happy, I . . . wander desolately back to that time of my life. . . . That I suffered in secret, and that I suffered exquisitely, no one ever knew but I.

Following a quarrel with John Dickens, Lamert fired Charles after twenty weeks that seemed to Charles like twenty years. The experience of the blacking factory made an indelible impression on him, setting in him a hard determination, but through his suffering he developed an equally permanent sensitivity from which he created in his novels a host of suffering children and other innocent victims of injustice and pain.

After three months in Marshalsea, John Dickens's mother died and John inherited £450, enough to get him out of prison, and John went back to his job with the navy. From 1824 to 1826, he sent Charles to Wellington House Academy, where Charles studied English, French, Latin, writing, mathematics, and dancing. When John lost his job and took work as a reporter for the *British Press,* he was again deep in debt, and Charles had to drop out of school. He took a job at the law office of Ellis and Blackmore, which he found so boring that he determined never to be a lawyer who spent his life "splitting hairs slowly and growing rich on the distress of others." Dickens then set out to educate himself. He taught himself shorthand in eighteen months, went to acting school, and procured a pass to the Reading Room in the British Museum (the national library) where he spent hours reading, the "usefullest [days] of my life."

DICKENS BEGINS AS A JOURNALIST

Four years after taking a law-clerk job, Dickens began his writing career as a reporter. Once he had mastered shorthand, he set himself up as a freelance reporter near the law courts and waited to be hired as a recorder of court cases. He acquired a job on the *Mirror of Parliament,* a paper that reported the daily transactions of the lawmakers, and worked his way to an advanced position hiring and supervising other reporters. He earned a reputation for accuracy and speed in recording speeches of members of Parliament, and was invited to join the staff of another paper, the *True Sun.* As a reporter observing the workings of Parliament, he was unimpressed with its red tape; he saw that a few reforms benefited the middle class, but that lawmakers did nothing for the masses of poor whose lives were, as he described, "misery, starvation, unemployment and cholera." Though he himself had acquired some professional and economic success, he still remembered the days in the blacking factory and had compassion for those who worked hard and had almost nothing.

While working at the law office, Dickens had met and fallen in love with Maria Beadnell, a banker's daughter a year older than he. Dickens pursued her diligently, but her parents disapproved. The disappointment of losing Maria renewed old feelings of despair and shame felt so vividly during the days of the blacking factory. At his twenty-first birthday party, Maria rejected him, after which Charles returned her letters, but she kept up a teasing relationship that fed his hopes. When Maria's parents sent her to Paris to finishing school, Charles realized he had no chance to win her love after four years of trying. He vowed he would never again be anyone's plaything. Lacking family wealth or prestige, he would need independent success, and from then on he was determined to have his way.

After 1833 Dickens's determination and hard work brought results. The *Morning Chronicle* hired him as a full-time reporter and soon after added him to the staff of its affiliate, the *Evening Chronicle*. When the *Monthly Magazine* printed, without his name and without paying him, a sketch Dickens had submitted, he was thrilled to see his writing in print. The editors asked for more sketches, which he signed "Boz" for the first time in 1834. Dickens took the name Boz from his family; his little brother Augustus, nicknamed Moses but unable to pronounce the word, called himself Boz. When Dickens was covering plays for the *Evening Chronicle,* he discovered that some of the Boz sketches had been adapted for the stage. Dickens's "sketches" were entertainingly written anecdotes about London people and places. Since the *Monthly Magazine* did not pay him, he quit and wrote street sketches for the *Evening Chronicle.* In addition, he wrote twelve sketches for *Bell's Life in London.* His new success brought him to the attention of writer William Harrison Ainsworth, who introduced Dickens to artist George Cruikshank and publisher John Macrone. In 1836, on Dickens's twenty-fourth birthday, Macrone published *Sketches by Boz,* a two-volume collection of sketches illustrated by Cruikshank.

George Hogarth, Dickens's editor on the *Evening Chronicle,* often invited Dickens to join family gatherings and introduced Dickens to his daughters, all of whom Dickens found charming. On April 2, 1836, he married the oldest daughter, Catherine, called Kate, at St. Luke's Church, Chelsea. When the couple was settled, Catherine's sixteen-year-old sister, Mary, came to live with them; unmarried sisters or brothers' living with a married couple was common practice in Dickens's day. Later, Dickens's brother Fred also lived in their home. Charles and Mary, who had a sweeter disposition than Catherine, developed a close friendship with more understanding than existed between Charles and his wife, who nevertheless bore ten children, seven boys and three girls, between 1837 and 1852.

FROM SKETCHES TO NOVELS

When *Sketches by Boz* brought good reviews, publishers Chapman and Hall invited Dickens to write, for £14 a month, twenty monthly installments about an imaginary sports club, the Nemrod Club, sketches to be illustrated by Robert Seymour. Dickens, knowing nothing about sports, renegotiated the proposal to focus instead on the travels and investigations of Mr. Pickwick and the imaginary Pickwick Club, illustrated by Hablôt Knight Browne, called Phiz, who became Dickens's illustrator for other works. The first installments from the Pickwick Club were poorly received, until Dickens added the character of Sam Weller in the fourth installment. The addition changed the fortunes of the series from sales of four thousand to forty thousand copies. Biographer Wolf Mankowitz describes the popularity of Pickwick:

> It was read upstairs and downstairs [by all classes], by judges on the bench and the cleaners after them. . . . Critics spoke of Dickens as another Cervantes, poor people shared a shilling copy and read it aloud in groups. A clergyman, having consoled a sick man, heard him mutter behind his back, "Well, thank God, Pickwick will be out in ten days anyway!"

Chapman and Hall sold back issues by the thousands, and they more than doubled Dickens's salary. The installments were published as a book, entitled *Pickwick Papers,* in 1837. Dickens was "the sudden lion of the town," and offers poured in for children's books, novels, and more sketches.

Dickens accepted an offer to edit the monthly *Bentley's Miscellany* and include in it installments of *Oliver Twist,* to be illustrated by Cruikshank, the illustrator of Boz. The first February 1837 installment garnered great reviews and sold many copies even though it had a more serious tone than *Pickwick.* In *Pickwick,* Dickens presented prison with humor and a mild view; in *Oliver Twist,* he wrote about prison in grave, realistic language. While he was writing the installments for the novel, Mary Hogarth died suddenly. Because Dickens loved Mary as a close friend, he felt such grief he had to take time off. He coped with the loss by taking long walks and horseback rides with John Forster, who had become his friend and agent. Dickens's sadness over Mary's death further strained his relationship with Catherine, who, though she mourned the loss of her sister, was jealous of her husband's affection for Mary. Determined to continue writing, he finished the installments, after which Bentley published *Oliver Twist* in a three-volume book in 1838, the first book to have Dickens's name, not the anonymous "Boz," on the title page.

Before Dickens completed *Oliver Twist* he was already thinking of his next novel, and he traveled with his illustrator Phiz to Yorkshire to research the conditions of boarding schools there. He found maggots, fleas, beatings, and ignorance, schools where illegitimate children were hidden for low fees. At Bowes Academy, run by one-eyed William Shaw, boys were sick, some went blind, and on average one died each year. These schools became the model for Dotheboys Hall in *Nicholas Nickleby*, whose first installment was published in April 1838 while Dickens was still drawing praise from critics for *Oliver Twist*. Of *Nicholas Nickleby*, biographer Edgar Johnson says, "it mingles the sunlight of *Pickwick* with the darkness of *Oliver*," and "fuses the inexhaustible laughter of *Pickwick* with the somber themes of *Oliver Twist*." These two books, *Oliver Twist* and *Nicholas Nickleby*, Johnson says, "were clarion peals announcing to the world that in Charles Dickens the rejected and forgotten and misused of the world had a champion." The first installment of *Nicholas Nickleby* sold fifty thousand copies on the first day.

The success of Dickens's books brought him enough earnings to move up in social class. He bought a house with a gate on Doughty Street in London and traveled within England and abroad. He was invited to join social clubs and literary societies and met other writers—essayist Leigh Hunt and novelists William Thackeray and Edward Bulwer-Lytton. Invitations came to Dickens from the city's cultured elite on the west end of town, but not to Kate, not known for charm or wit. Dickens was greeted by footmen and led up grand staircases to attend breakfasts and dinners at which the educated and famous displayed their skills and amused one another. Mankowitz describes Dickens's reaction to this social class:

> It was a strictly mannered, often cruel world, but Dickens had already learned self-assurance, was a practised mimic of any tone, and felt confident in his intelligence and great gifts:

gifts, he soon came to realize, that few of these privileged people had even a tiny part of. That awareness defended him against their insolence or patronization. He was acute enough to see behind the social masks.

As Mankowitz says, Dickens's novels harshly satirize the "masters of material gain and the parasites of materialism, in law courts, the factories and workhouses," but they seldom attack the aristocratic and intellectual elite. He became adviser to one of its members, Angela Burdett Coutts, an heiress who wanted to use money from her two fortunes for social improvement. She took Dickens's advice to fund slum clearance and homes for "fallen women."

Though Dickens's social relations went smoothly, his relations with critics and publishers were often rancorous. Writing about *Oliver Twist*, one critic said that Dickens wrote so much and so fast that he was likely to decline in quality and popularity unless he slowed down. Dickens, angered, vowed, "They shall eat their words." G.K. Chesterton thought perhaps the critics misunderstood Dickens and said, "Dickens has greatly suffered with the critics precisely through this stunning simplicity in his best work," but his disputes with publishers usually involved money and contracts, not the quality of his work. Dickens was inclined to sign a contract that seemed good at the time, then demand more money than the original contract stipulated when sales and the publisher's profits were much larger than expected. In one dispute with the publisher Bentley, Dickens wanted both money and a change in the work contract. Bentley had published *Oliver Twist*, and contracted with Dickens for two additional novels. Dickens wanted to consider *Oliver Twist* one of the two and then jump to the publishers Chapman and Hall. When the dispute reached a stalemate, Dickens's friend and agent Forster negotiated for him. The determination Dickens had learned from the days at the blacking factory got him what he wanted but left hard feelings with the publisher that Forster was unable to smooth over.

LITTLE NELL SAVES A WEEKLY

Dickens wanted to be free of the contract with Bentley because he had an idea for a weekly that he wanted Chapman and Hall to fund. Dickens intended *Master Humphrey's Clock* to include a variety of short sketches written by a number of contributors. Responding to the sale of seventy thousand copies of the first issue, Dickens said, "What will the wiseacres say to weekly issues *now*? and what will they say to any of those ten thousand things we shall do together to make 'em writhe and stagger in their shoes." Sales, however, dropped markedly when the public discovered the weekly had no installments by Dickens. Within two weeks, Dickens was serializing *The Old Curiosity Shop,* a travel story about an odd collection of characters. In *The World of Charles Dickens,* Angus Wilson says that this novel

> shows up alarmingly to modern readers the degree of oddity then accepted in a supposedly realistic story—a devilish, fire-drinking dwarf, a little child, an undersized servant maid, a woman (Sally Brass), who is reported as having enlisted as a guardsman or gone down to the docks in male attire, a small boy who stands on his head in mudflats.

It was, however, sweet Little Nell, persecuted by the dwarf Quilp and loved by the honest boy Kit Nubbles, who captured readers' hearts and sent weekly sales above a hundred thousand copies. When Nell neared death, readers deluged the paper with letters pleading that Dickens not let her die. Die she did, nonetheless, in an installment that prompted an outpouring of emotion, as Mankowitz describes:

> Scottish critic Lord Jeffrey was found weeping in his library. 'I'm a great goose to have given way so', he sobbed, 'but I couldn't help it.' [Actor William] Macready, [playwright and poet Walter] Landor, Thomas Carlyle and Edgar Allan Poe were all moved to a similar plight. So was [member of Parliament] Daniel O'Connell, reading on a train journey; he groaned, 'He should not have killed her', and threw the story out of the window.

Dickens's hold on the attention and sentiment of the public loosened with the weekly installments of his next novel written for *Master Humphrey's Clock.* A historical novel, *Barnaby Rudge* recounts the riots of the poor against Parliament, but Dickens gives the story a more anti-Catholic than anti-Parliament emphasis. The strain of producing weekly installments of two books took a toll on Dickens's health, and he took a year's rest, which publishers Chapman and Hall funded with a salary.

DICKENS'S VISIT TO AMERICA

During his year off, Dickens and Catherine visited America. They sailed on January 2, 1842, and arrived in Boston to huge crowds wanting to know why Little Nell had to die. He and Catherine visited Boston, Niagara, Philadelphia,

St. Louis, and New York City. Wherever he went, crowds surrounded him, cheered, stared, wrung his hand, and clipped fur souvenirs from his coat. He had invitations from every state, from universities, Congress, and all kinds of public and private bodies. He visited orphanages, schools for the blind, reform schools, prisons, and industrial mills. New York published a special edition, the *Extra Boz Herald*, and held a Boz Ball in a ballroom decorated with characters from his books. In a letter to Forster, Dickens wrote:

> I can do nothing that I want to do, go nowhere where I want to go, and see nothing that I want to see. If I turn into the street, I am followed by a multitude. If I stay at home, the house becomes, with callers, like a fair. . . . If I go to a party in the evening, and am so enclosed and hedged about by people, stand where I will, that I am exhausted for want of air. I go to church for quiet, and there is a violent rush to the neighbourhood of the pew I sit in, and the clergyman preaches at *me*. I take my seat in a railroad car, and the very conductor won't leave me alone. I get out at a station, and can't drink a glass of water, without having a hundred people looking down my throat when I open my mouth to swallow. . . . I have no peace, and am in a perpetual worry.

In Washington, D.C., Dickens attended a session of Congress and visited President Tyler, who said little and sat beside a spitoon. To Dickens's amazement, people everywhere—in offices of the state, in courts of law, at parties, in bars, on trains—chewed large wads of tobacco and spit everywhere, "all squirted forth upon the carpet a yellow saliva which quite altered the pattern." Dickens's patience gradually ran out. At one dinner in his honor, after being introduced as a moral reformer and a champion of the downtrodden, Dickens began speaking in the manner expected of him, but midway in his remarks, he switched to the topic of American copyright laws and railed against the unfairness of Americans who made a profit from his works and those of Sir Walter Scott without paying the authors anything. The audience applauded politely, but the next day's papers criticized him for insulting those who had come to honor him. American authors remained silent on the subject, a situation that baffled and rankled Dickens. G.K. Chesterton comments on the English misunderstanding of Americans:

> America is a mystery to any good Englishman; but I think Dickens managed somehow to touch it on a queer nerve. There is one thing, at any rate, . . . that while there is no materialism so crude or so material as American materialism, there is also no idealism so crude or so ideal as American

idealism. America will always affect an Englishman as being soft in the wrong place and hard in the wrong place. . . . Some beautiful ideal runs through this people, but it runs aslant.

After four months of tours, crowds, and little privacy, Dickens left New York harbor on June 7, 1842, to sail for home, his children and friends, and his writing.

Before beginning his next novel, Dickens recorded his impressions of his American visit in *American Notes.* In polite tones, he praised many features of American life (and remained silent about copyright laws). America had, however, failed to live up to Dickens's expectations; its slavery, its business practices, its sensational journalism, and the manners of its people offended him. The book brought Dickens £1,000 toward the cost of the trip, but it brought him an array of adjectives in American newspapers—"coarse, vulgar, impudent, superficial, narrow-minded, conceited cockney, flimsy, childish, trashy, contemptible." He was less polite in his next book. After several installments of *Martin Chuzzlewit* sold poorly, Dickens hoped to increase sales by sending Martin to America. With none of the polite restraint shown in *American Notes,* Dickens expressed his impatience with America in harsh humor through the character of Mrs. Gamp, a brutalized victim of the society in which Mr. Pecksniff rules with unctuous hypocrisy. The Americans were angry, the British disappointed by its bitter tone, and Dickens's publishers reduced his year-off salary.

RESTLESSNESS AND TRAVEL

The year following his American visit, 1843, began a period of restlessness for Dickens. In a row with Chapman and Hall over salary, Dickens lost his temper and threatened to find a new publisher, but Christmas was coming soon and he did not act. Instead, with financial pressures mounting—*Chuzzlewit* sales had been disappointing and household expenses were growing—Dickens threw himself into writing a Christmas story. Working at a feverish pace, he completed the manuscript, originally titled *A Christmas Carol, In Prose, Being a Ghost Story of Christmas,* by the end of November. It was published shortly before Christmas 1843. With its attractive gold-lettered cover and hand-colored interior illustrations, six thousand copies were sold the first day. It was not just the physical beauty of the book that drew praise. Like readers today, Dickens's contemporaries were deeply moved by the story's message that Christmas can and should spread love and brotherhood among humanity.

Dickens was exceedingly pleased with his Christmas story and its huge sales. Yet the book didn't generate as substantial an income for Dickens as he had hoped. With its colored plates, the book was costly to produce. At the same time, the selling price was fixed at only five shillings, leaving little profit for the author. Dickens was incensed. Although he never used color plates again, he would go on to write in the new genre that he had created: the Christmas book.

During this time, Georgina Hogarth, daughter of George Hogarth, who was as sweet as Mary had been, came to live in the Dickens home. After the holidays, Dickens took his family and servants to Italy, stopping first in Genoa and renting a house from which he could hear Genoa's constantly chiming bells. He used the opportunity to write another Christmas story, entitled "The Chimes," which became the second in a series of annual Christmas stories. In the following years, he wrote "The Cricket on the Hearth," "The Battle of Life," and "The Haunted Man" for publication just before the holidays. Before returning to England, he and Kate toured southern Italy, where he came to appreciate the manners and language of the Italians but grew to dislike the Catholic Church, which was, he thought, "a political arm against the poor and ignorant." Unlike his American trip, this trip was private and much more satisfying. When he returned to England in 1846, he started a new liberal paper, *Daily News,* during a political turmoil over the Corn Laws. When the first issue came off the press, ten thousand Londoners wanted to see what Dickens had said, as did thousands around the rest of the country. But once the paper was successfully established, Dickens lost patience with the details of publication and turned it over to Forster after seventeen issues.

Dickens became a familiar figure in London and a comic but difficult character in his home. A man of medium height who appeared small, he had thick brown hair, a mustache and beard, a large expressive mouth, and bright, active eyes that darted back and forth, taking in the details around him. His nervous and delicate manner belied a rather steely personality. He wore flashy waistcoats and velvet coats in public and liked to be looked at if the looks were admiring. Personally, he fussed over little things and directed his whims to be acted on instantly: If the house was too quiet at night, everyone had to get up; if it was too noisy, all had to be quiet. G.K. Chesterton said of Dickens, "His private life consisted of one tragedy and ten thousand comedies." His marriage was a failure, but he loved his children, and filled their home with energy, with daily pranks and practical jokes.

PERSONAL AND PROFESSIONAL TURNING POINTS

The mid-1840s marked a turning point both in Dickens's personal life and in his novels. Unhappy in his marriage, he developed undisciplined and unhealthy habits in his daily routines. His discontent spurred him to go to Lausanne, Switzerland, to start a new novel, *Dombey and Son*, his last farce. Like all of Dickens's first novels, which are primarily farces, *Dombey* is filled with caricatures who could not exist anywhere; the novels that followed have more realistic characters who could live everywhere. *Dombey* attacks the class system and moral pestilence that Dickens believed corrupted English society. He believed that the aristocracy perpetuated itself by taking advantage of "the pure, weak good nature" of the people.

If *Dombey* is the last of the first novels, *David Copperfield* is the transition novel. Dickens got the idea for the title by reversing his initials. It is his most autobiographical book and his favorite, about which he said, "I really think I have done it ingeniously and with a very complicated interweaving of truth and fiction." He tells the story of David in the first person and makes memory an important part of the theme, memories so personal that at one point he temporarily stopped writing because he felt sick and weak and shed tears for days. Writing *David Copperfield* helped to heal some of Dickens's wounds: "I can never approach the book with perfect composure it had such perfect possession of me when I wrote it." From the first installment in May 1849, the book was a success with the public. Novelist William Thackeray said, "By jingo it's beautiful. . . . Those inimitable Dickens touches which make such a great man of him. . . . There are little words and phrases in his book that are like personal benefits to his readers. . . . Bravo Dickens." And yet after the successful completion of this novel, Dickens was still restless and filled with nervous energy, which he directed toward production of plays.

As early as 1836, Dickens was interested in plays, but he had little success as a dramatist. His interest continued, however, in the form of amateur theatricals, farces Dickens and his family performed for friends at annual Twelfth Night celebrations in his home. Each year these productions became more elaborate until he offered them publicly and used the profits for charity. In 1847 he organized a theatrical company for his charity plays, arranged a benefit tour of the play *Every Man in His Humor,* and gave the profits to a budding but poor playwright. The next year the company produced *The Merry Wives of Windsor* to buy Shakespeare's birthplace in Stratford-on-Avon as a national monument. As the production of charity plays grew and audiences increased, Dickens hired professional actresses Mary Boyle and Ellen Ternan. In 1852 the company performed in thirteen cities and put on a performance for Queen Victoria, all profits going to the Guild of Literature and Art.

Amid his busy schedule of writing books and producing plays, Dickens leased a larger house in Tavistock Square in a more fashionable area of London, but first contracted to reconstruct, redecorate, and refurnish it before the family moved in. While waiting for the work to be done, he was too agitated to work; he said, "I sit down between whiles to think of a new story, and, as it begins to grow, such a torment of desire to be anywhere but where I am . . . takes hold of me, that it is like being *driven away.*" He settled down, however, after he had moved into the Tavistock home and started *Bleak House.* The first novel of the second, more realistic phase, *Bleak House* centers around a legal issue that typified the way the courts handled cases for prisoners of Chancery. Dickens parallels the slow pace of the courts to the coming and going of the indifferent political parties, satirically called Boodle and Coodle. From the first chapter, fog covers the whole London world of Chancery, the dark, murky atmosphere in which Dickens exposes the corruptions and ineptitudes of government and the courts. The first issue of *Bleak House* exceeded the sales of *David Copperfield* by ten thousand copies.

In 1850 Dickens started and edited a weekly called *Household Words,* a publication of short articles and tidbits written by a variety of contributors. Though Dickens exercised firm control over the editing of contributors' work, he gave many young writers an opportunity for valuable training. Subject matter covered a wide range: public education, campaigns against social abuses, entertainment, fiction, and humor. Two weeks after its first issue, a monthly news supplement was added, the *Household Narrative of Current Events.* The weekly carried explanations of scientific and technological discoveries, brief biographies of many historical figures, reviews of new and old books, travel tips, and Dickens's installments of *A Child's History of England.* Since three out of four people in England could read, Dickens wanted the weekly to appeal to all social classes. When circulation began to decline after more than two years of regular publication, Dickens propped up sales with a new book, *Hard Times,* in which he uses places to portray two opposing views. Coketown represents cold, rational industrialism and the Circus represents warmth, intuition, and humanity; in the end, the natural world of Sissy Jupe and the Circus people is the only hope. Before writing this book about the materialistic laws of supply and demand, the system of high profits and cheap labor preached by utilitarians, Dickens toured the cotton mills of Lancashire and interviewed striking cotton workers in Preston.

PUBLIC SUCCESS AND PRIVATE SADNESS

As a result of the reforms Dickens advocated in *Household Words,* he was sought as a public speaker and lecturer; out of these appearances he developed public readings from his works. He began with readings of "A Christmas Carol" and donated the proceeds to poor workers. He added other works, cut the excerpts and wrote stage directions, and took his readings throughout England, Scotland, and Ireland to audiences up to two thousand. Though he did not need the money and the exertion of performance strained his health, he liked the stimulation he received from the audiences. The next year, he hired a personal valet and an agent to help him with forty-two performances in Birmingham and Ireland. In 1867 he planned a hundred readings for an American tour. He had large, sell-out audiences in Boston, New York, Philadelphia, Baltimore, and Washington. But after seventy-six performances, Dickens's health was failing and he had to go home. In 1868 he went on a farewell reading tour in London, Ireland, and Scotland, but grew more and more exhausted with each performance. His agent Dolby, who urged him to quit, described Dickens as a man with "the iron will of a demon and the tender pity of an angel." At every reading, Dickens insisted that a certain number of good seats be sold for a small amount to the poor, believing that those he had spent his life championing should be able to hear what he said.

For many years, Dickens's public life had been a series of successes, but his private life was marked by numerous sad events. In 1848 his sister Fanny died of tuberculosis, followed by the death of her crippled son. Following the birth of their third daughter, Kate had a nervous breakdown. Shortly after Kate recovered, Dickens's father, John, died, and the baby, Dora Annie, became ill and died before she was a year old. Over the years, Dickens's relationship with Kate had continued to deteriorate, and when Dickens flirted with other women and gave them his attention, Kate, cowed by her famous and brilliant husband, withdrew further. During one of the public-reading tours, Kate left him. Dickens blamed himself:

> It is not only that she makes me uneasy and unhappy, but that I make her so too—and much more so . . . but we are strangely ill-assorted for the bond there is between us. God knows she would have been a thousand times happier if she had married another kind of man, and that her avoidance of this destiny would have been at least equally good for us both. I am often cut to the heart by thinking what a pity it is, for her own sake, that I ever fell in her way.

When Kate left with one of the children, Georgina Hogarth stayed on and ran the household as she had been doing for some years. In addition to his other problems, several of Dickens's brothers, who managed money as irresponsibly as their father had done, asked Dickens for financial help. While personal problems made him impatient and irritable, they never depleted his energy and enthusiasm for his work.

Dickens's whirlwind of plays, readings, serials, family, friends, travels, and new houses never seemed to die down. By chance, Dickens learned that he could buy Gad's Hill, the "castle" from his childhood, when he discovered that one of the contributors to *Household Words*, Eliza Lynn, owned it and wanted to sell. "I used to look at it [Gad's Hill] as a wonderful Mansion (which God knows it is not), when I was a very odd little child with the first faint shadows of all my books in my head," he said. He had it renovated and enlarged and brought his family there for the summer of 1857. Dickens was spending more of his time with younger people now—his children, the staff of *Household Words*, and actors from the charity plays. He particularly enjoyed a friendship with Wilkie Collins, a young writer on the staff, and traveled with him to the Lake District and Paris. And his attraction to young Ellen Ternan, with whom he had acted in many plays, grew to serious infatuation.

NEW NOVELS FOR THE MAGAZINES

Dickens's major accomplishment in the last two decades of his life was the writing of six novels and part of a seventh that constitute the second phase of his career. After *Bleak House* and *Hard Times* came *Little Dorrit,* a serial novel in which Dickens attacks the cynicism, despair, and victim attitude that existed in all levels of society. It has few saints and few villains but many gray characters—bad people with redeeming qualities and good people with sinister motives. Little Dorrit, whose girlhood is affected, as Dickens's was, by a father imprisoned for debts, grows up to lead a useful, happy life. Before writing another novel, Dickens had a fight with his publisher of fourteen years, Bradbury and Evans. In the outcome, Dickens took *Household Words,* renamed it *All the Year Round,* and went back to publishers Chapman and Hall. The first serial novel published in the renamed weekly was *A Tale of Two Cities,* Dickens's story version of Thomas Carlyle's account of the French Revolution and the last book illustrated by Phiz. In this book, Dickens explores the theme of renunciation, redemption, and resurrection through the character of Sydney Carton, who offers to die in a convicted man's place.

A year later, Dickens explores the same theme of renunciation, redemption, and resurrection in *Great Expectations.* The main character, Pip, goes from the country to London and back, during which he meets eccentric characters and discovers that multiple strands of his life are interwoven. During the interim between *Great Expectations* and Dickens's next novel, Chapman and Hall published a collection of pieces from *All the Year Round* entitled *The Uncommercial Traveller,* the same title used for a second collection four years later. The next novel, *Our Mutual Friend,* appeared in monthly installments for a year and a half, beginning in May 1864. It is a modern novel, set in Dickens's mid-Victorian England, in which he anticipates the nature of declining Victorianism. He portrays a society so corrupt that money, which Dickens symbolizes as huge dustheaps, has become the measure of human worth. Angus Wilson says of *Our Mutual Friend,* "What is so extraordinary is that the tired Dickens should so nearly capture this world of the future, this world only glimpsed by a few beneath the seeming-solid surface of the sixties." The last novel, *The Mystery of Edwin Drood,* set in a small cathedral town, involves the upper-middle, professional class. In the six parts that Dickens wrote before he died, there is an unsolved murder, and critics have argued that its theme involves the forces of law against evil.

DECLINING HEALTH AND DEATH

Dickens's health was in decline for the last five years of his life. After a mild stroke in 1865, he drove himself to exhaustion on his reading tours. In March 1870, he gave his final public reading at St. James Hall. At the end, when his voice weakened, two thousand people rose to their feet, and he returned to the stage. Tears falling down his cheeks, he said, "From these garish lights I now vanish for ever more, with a heartfelt, grateful, respectful, affectionate farewell," and he kissed his hands to the audience and was gone. In late spring, he went to Gad's Hill to work on *Edwin Drood,* but he seemed to know the end was near when he told his daughter Katey on her last visit that he had high hopes for the book if he lived to finish it. On June 8, he worked all day rather than following his usual routine of working only in the morning. When he stood up from the dinner table that evening, he collapsed and was put on the sofa. He lay quietly, breathing heavily, until six o'clock the next evening, June 9, 1870, when he died at the age of fifty-eight. On June 14, his body was brought to Westminster Abbey, and after a simple service, he was laid to rest in Poet's Corner, a section of the church where honored writers are buried. Thousands of people filed past the grave left open for the public until it was full to overflowing with flowers.

CHARACTERS AND PLOT

LIST OF CHARACTERS

Bob Cratchit: The impoverished clerk who is harshly treated by his employer, Ebenezer Scrooge; head of the Cratchit family.

Martha Cratchit: The eldest Cratchit daughter; she works as an apprentice for a milliner.

Mrs. Cratchit: Bob's wife, who lovingly cares for the family's six children.

Fan: Scrooge's dead younger sister, and mother of Fred.

Fezziwig: The benevolent businessman for whom Scrooge, in his younger years, worked as an apprentice.

Fred: Scrooge's good-natured nephew; he invites Scrooge to dine with him on Christmas.

Ghost of Christmas Future: The dark, hooded ghost that shows Scrooge shadows of the things that have not yet happened, but that will happen if Scrooge's course remains unaltered.

Ghost of Christmas Past: The ghost that appears to be half child and half man; it shows Scrooge scenes from his past.

Ghost of Christmas Present: The hearty, generous ghost described as a "jolly Giant, glorious to see"; it reveals scenes as they unfold in present time.

Jacob Marley: Scrooge's business partner in life; Marley's ghost foreshadows Scrooge's haunting by three Christmas spirits.

Ebenezer Scrooge: The miserly protagonist who learns kindness and forbearance when he is haunted by three Spirits.

Tiny Tim: Bob Cratchit's crippled young son.

Dick Wilkins: Young Scrooge's friend and fellow apprentice at Fezziwig's warehouse.

PLOT SUMMARY

The *Carol* is framed within twenty-four hours of Scrooge's life, which Dickens divides into five staves, or parts.

Stave One: Marley's Ghost

Before the story begins to unfold, the Narrator tells the reader that Ebenezer Scrooge's business partner Jacob Marley is "as dead as a door-nail." Their firm was known as "Scrooge and Marley" and even though Marley has been dead for seven years, Scrooge never bothered to paint out Marley's name above the warehouse door; now, in Marley's absence, Scrooge answers to both names.

Describing Scrooge, the Narrator exclaims: "Oh! But he was a tight-fisted hand at the grindstone, was Scrooge! A squeezing, wrenching, grasping, scraping, clutching, covetous old sinner! External heat and cold had little influence on him. No warmth could warm, no cold could chill him. No wind that blew was bitterer than he, no falling snow was more intent upon his purpose."

The story opens on a biting cold, foggy Christmas Eve. Scrooge sits busy in his counting house. He watches his clerk, Bob Cratchit, who tries in vain to warm himself in the dismal office adjacent to Scrooge's. Suddenly, Scrooge's nephew Fred bursts into the office. His cheerful proclamations of "Merry Christmas" are rebuked by Scrooge's angry words: "Bah! Humbug!" In his tirade against Christmas, Scrooge calls the holiday nothing but "a time for paying bills without money," and "a time for finding yourself a year older, and not an hour richer." Fred counters this acrid interpretation, calling Christmas a "good time . . . a kind, forgiving, charitable, pleasant time." When he invites his uncle to Christmas dinner, Scrooge resolutely declines.

As Scrooge's nephew departs from Scrooge's office, two portly gentlemen arrive. In their endeavor to assist the poor during the holiday season, they entreat Scrooge to make a monetary donation. Scrooge suggests instead that the destitute be sent to prisons and workhouses, establishments that Scrooge himself supports.

Meanwhile, outside, the fog and cold intensify. A young boy stops before Scrooge's shop to sing a Christmas carol, but Scrooge rebuffs him with such vehemence that the young singer flees in terror.

Upon closing time, Scrooge chastises his clerk for wanting Christmas day off. He reluctantly agrees to give Cratchit the day, but not before calling Christmas "a poor excuse for picking a man's pocket every twenty-fifth of December!"

Scrooge goes home to the gloomy chambers that once had been home to his deceased partner Marley. As he unlocks the front door, Scrooge imagines that he sees the image of Marley's face in the door knocker. Taking more precaution than usual, Scrooge inspects the interior of his home and double locks the doors. Now outfitted in his dressing gown and retired to the fire, the astonished Scrooge beholds a disused bell begin to ring. Other bells begin to ring; the clamor is succeeded by a deep clanking noise. Then, before Scrooge's eyes, a frightful specter, dragging heavy chains, of Jacob Marley passes into the room. The apparition informs Scrooge that "it is required of every man that the spirit within him should walk abroad among his fellow-men, and travel far and wide; and if that spirit goes not forth in life, it is condemned to do so after death." Thus, Marley explains, because he did not use his mortal life well—did not exercise charity, mercy, forbearance, and benevolence toward his fellow man—his weary spirit is doomed to walk the earth, fettered with the chains he forged in life. Marley warns Scrooge that he will be haunted by three ghosts and that through their visits, he can escape Marley's dreadful fate. As Marley floats out into the dark night, Scrooge sees that the sky is filled with phantoms. Each one wears chains like those fettering Marley. As the images fade, Scrooge retreats to his bed and falls instantly asleep.

Stave Two: The First of the Three Spirits
Scrooge awakens in total darkness. As the church clock tolls one, light flashes into the room and a strange figure parts his bed curtains. The apparition looks both like a child and an old man—its hair is white with age yet its skin has not the crease of a single wrinkle. From its head springs a bright jet of light. The Spirit proclaims itself the "Ghost of Christmas Past."

When Scrooge touches the Spirit's hand, the two pass through the wall and arrive out in a countryside that is familiar to Scrooge. It is Christmastime. The Spirit takes Scrooge to the dismal schoolhouse where he sees a solitary figure—himself as a boy—engrossed in a book. Scrooge weeps to see "his poor forgotten self as he used to be." The Spirit shows Scrooge another Christmas, one in which Scrooge is still a boy at the school, though older. Scrooge watches as his younger sister Fan enters the school and showers her forlorn brother with hugs and kisses. She declares that she has come to take Scrooge home.

Scrooge grows excited when the Spirit takes him to another scene from his past: the warehouse where the youthful Scrooge was apprenticed. Scrooge recognizes the jovial
image of his former boss, whom he calls Old Fezziwig, and
also his friend Dick Wilkins. Scrooge watches as his younger
self and Dick clear out the warehouse in preparation for
Christmas Eve festivities. The entire Fezziwig family arrives,
along with the other young men and women employed by
Fezziwig. A fiddler's music fills the makeshift ballroom;
great clapping and joyful dancing ensue. The merry revelers
consume huge pieces of meats, cakes, and mince-pies, along
with plenty of beer. When the party breaks up, Scrooge comments that Fezziwig "had the power to render us happy or
unhappy; to make our service light or burdensome; a pleasure or a toil." He notes, too, that he should like to be able to
say a word or two to Bob Cratchit.

At the Spirit's prompting, Scrooge sees another image of
his former self. He is older now, sitting next to a young girl
with tearful eyes. To Scrooge she cries, "Another idol has displaced me . . . a golden one. . . . I have seen your nobler
aspirations fall off one by one, until the master-passion,
Gain, engrosses you." She goes on to release the young
Scrooge from his commitment to her, a "dowerless girl."
Deeply disturbed by these images of what have been,
Scrooge implores the Spirit to haunt him no longer. The
Spirit is relentless, however, and forces Scrooge to witness
one more scene. This time, as Scrooge watches his former
betrothed with her husband and beautiful daughter, he re-
flects that he might have enjoyed the comforts of family had
he chosen a different path. Exhausted, Scrooge is barely
conscious of being back in his own bedroom before he sinks
into a deep sleep.

Stave Three: The Second of the Three Spirits
Scrooge awakens in his bedroom. As he shuffles into his sitting room he finds it transformed: A roaring fire fills the
hearth and the room is bedecked with holly and mistletoe.
Heaped on the floor are huge amounts of food, including
succulent turkeys and geese, and a great array of plum
puddings, chestnuts, and luscious fruits. Upon the couch sits
a giant who bears a glowing torch. It calls itself the Ghost of
Christmas Present.

First, the Spirit conducts Scrooge to the city streets on
Christmas morning. They observe the cheerful bustle as the

townspeople prepare for their festivities. Next, the two visit Bob Cratchit's small, four-roomed home. Mrs. Cratchit and the Cratchit children busily prepare for the Christmas feast as Martha, the eldest Cratchit daughter, arrives home. To fool her father, Martha hides herself just as Bob Cratchit, carrying his crippled son Tiny Tim, comes in the door. When he is informed that Martha is not coming for Christmas, he is so disappointed that Martha comes out prematurely from her hiding place. After hugging his daughter, Bob relates to his wife Tiny Tim's thoughtful proclamation coming home that "he hoped the people saw him in the church, because he was a cripple, and it might be pleasant to them to remember, upon Christmas day, who made lame beggars walk and blind men see."

As Tiny Tim settles onto his stool by the fire, Master Peter and the two young Cratchits fetch the family's Christmas goose from the poultry shop. The entire family bustles about the snug home in preparation for dinner. The scene is happy as the Cratchits gather around the table, where they unabashedly delight in the roasted goose and steaming plum pudding. After dinner, with chestnuts crackling noisily, the family sits around a roaring fire, where Tiny Tim declares, "God bless us every one!" A shadow seems to descend upon the room, however, when Bob drinks to the health of Mr. Scrooge. At the very mention of his name, an enlivened Mrs. Cratchit calls her husband's employer an "odious, stingy, hard, unfeeling man."

As the Cratchits' revelry resumes several minutes later, the scene vanishes and Scrooge finds himself visiting other Christmas gatherings. Soon, Scrooge finds himself at the home of his nephew, who is enjoying the happy comradery of friends and family. The group laughs heartily when Fred recounts that Scrooge had called Christmas a "humbug." As they converse and play games into the evening, the party continues to mock Scrooge's disagreeable nature.

Suddenly, the Spirit and Scrooge are travelling again. They visit many scenes of misery: sick beds, almshouses, hospitals, and jails, but each is marked by a happy ending. Later, Scrooge sees something protruding from the Spirit's robes: a boy and a girl who appear "abject, frightful, hideous, miserable." Scrooge—appalled by their wretchedness—listens as the Spirit exclaims: "This boy is Ignorance. This girl is Want. Beware of them both, and all of their degree, but most of all beware this boy, for on his brow I see that written which is Doom, unless the writing be erased."

As the bell strikes twelve, Scrooge sees a solemn, hooded figure advancing toward him.

Stave Four: The Last of the Spirits
Scrooge realizes that the menacing figure is the Ghost of Christmas Yet to Come. Although he fears the Spirit, Scrooge acknowledges that he is prepared to bear its company so that he can learn to lead a better life. Suddenly, they are in the city, and Scrooge overhears a group of merchants conversing about the death of a person who remains unnamed.

The Spirit takes Scrooge to an obscure and filthy part of town. They observe a ragged group laughing at some items that they have stolen from a dead man, who as before remains unidentified. The group shows no feeling for the deceased as they compare their bounty, which includes sheets, towels, and bed curtains. The scene changes as the Spirit shows Scrooge a bare, uncurtained bed, on which, beneath a ragged sheet, lies a corpse. Although the Spirit points toward the head, Scrooge—deeply shaken—refuses to unveil the body.

The Spirit takes Scrooge to the Cratchit home. Mrs. Cratchit and the children sit by the fire; Scrooge notices that the usually boisterous children are very quiet. Little Tiny Tim has died. Bob arrives home and, heartbroken for his lost child, breaks into sobs.

Finally, the Spirit conveys Scrooge to a ruinous, neglected churchyard. The Spirit stands among the graves and points to a single headstone. It reads EBENEZER SCROOGE. Scrooge, horrified, cries out, "I am not the man I was. I will not be the man I must have been but for this intercourse. . . . Assure me that I yet may change these shadows you have shown me, by an altered life!" Although the Spirit does not answer him, Scrooge promises to keep Christmas in his heart and to remember the lessons he has learned.

Stave Five: The End of It
Scrooge finds himself at home in bed. He runs to the window and calls down to a boy, who informs Scrooge that it is Christmas Day. Scrooge sends the boy to purchase a huge turkey and deliver it to the Cratchits. Then, dressing himself in his finest clothes, Scrooge sets out upon the city streets. He is exceedingly pleasant to everyone around him. In the afternoon, he visits his nephew's home, where he enjoys a "wonderful party, wonderful games, wonderful unanimity, wonderful happiness!"

The next morning at the office, Scrooge catches Bob Cratchit arriving late for work. Bob fears he will be harshly reprimanded; instead, Scrooge tells his clerk that he is raising his salary. He also promises to assist the struggling Cratchit family. True to his word, Scrooge becomes a second father to Tiny Tim, who does not die. Having learned to keep Christmas in his heart, Scrooge becomes "as good a friend, as good a master, and as good a man, as the good old city knew, or any other good old city, town, or borough, in the good old world."

CHAPTER 1

Design and Imagery in *A Christmas Carol*

The Function of Time

Robert L. Patten

"*A Christmas Carol* is about time," writes Robert L. Patten, who argues that the multiplicity of time presented by Dickens is central to Scrooge's conversion. In the following essay, Patten identifies five kinds of time used by Dickens as a device to impart meaning and power to the *Carol:* chronological time, circular or recurrent time, time measured by the span of a human life, time after death, and historical time. The following essay is excerpted from an article Patten contributed to *Dickens Studies Annual.*

In the work of neither Dickens nor Trollope . . . is there any of what we might call "metaphysical" concern with time. Both authors, of course, were signally unintellectual and uninterested in such matters.

—John Henry Raleigh,
"The English Novel and the Three Kinds of Time"

We may call books fictive models of the temporal world.
—Frank Kermode, *The Sense of an Ending*

Contributing to the emotional power of the *Carol* is its brevity. Dickens later apologized for the "narrow space within which it was necessary to confine these Christmas Stories when they were originally published," alleging that it "rendered their construction a matter of some difficulty, and almost necessitated what is peculiar in their machinery." By narrow space, he refers to the format which, after the *Carol,* became standard for his, and many other authors' Christmas Books, tales short enough to be sold for a modest price, five shillings. But space and time are intimately connected for Dickens as professional writer: the major novels are not only longer, occupying more pages or space, but also were composed *and read* over a longer period of time. The difficulties he experienced in trying to compress a conversion into the shorter compass of *Hard Times* and *Great Expecta-*

Excerpted from "Dickens Time and Again," by Robert L. Patten, in *Dickens Studies Annual* vol. 2, edited by Robert B. Partlow (Carbondale: Southern Illinois University Press, 1972). Reprinted with permission of AMS Press, Inc.

tions are well known; in the longer works, he was able to take a more leisurely, and realistic, course.

The reference to "realistic" leads us to a second observation. The *Carol* was written in little over six weeks, beginning around the thirteenth of October; its effect was thus compressed for Dickens, as he compressed it for his readers by inventing "what is peculiar in their machinery," namely, the Ghosts. Ghost stories are a feature of English Christmases, as we can see in *Pickwick* and *The Turn of the Screw.* But the Ghosts are seasonally relevant in more complex and profound ways, because three of them are not the spirits of dead persons, but of Christmases Past, Present, and Yet to Come.

Framed within the twenty-four hours in Scrooge's fictional life the *Carol* recreates at least five past times, a fictive present from Christmas morning through Twelfth Night, and a potential future encompassing the deaths of Tiny Tim and Scrooge himself. The multiplicity of the story's temporal dimensions points up its central concern, a concern that is *adumbrated* by its peculiar machinery, for the *Carol* is about Time: Scrooge's conversion is effected, in multiple ways, by the agency of Time itself. And the whole story is an exposition of the meaning of Christmas Time—a book published at Christmas (17 December), about a Christmas Eve and Christmas Day, to be read, as it has been for over a century, as a kind of Christmas ritual. Its time is as close to that of its audience as the Ghosts are to Scrooge or the narrator to his readers, and he is "standing in the spirit at your elbow."

CALENDAR TIME

The variety of kinds of time present in the opening staves establishes its complex, and multiple, values. The simplest concept of time is that demarcated by calendars, Scrooge's own reliable repeater, and apparently—though not actually—by the chimes of the neighboring church. Regular and unremitting, this time can be counted on to persevere in its accustomed rhythm, day after day, night after night, until, unaccountably, on Christmas morning, having gone to bed after two in the morning Scrooge hears the heavy church bell toll midnight. Unsettled, he first assumes that the clock is wrong: "An icicle must have got into the works." His repeater confirms the preposterous hour. "It isn't possible that anything has happened to the sun," he speculates, "and this is twelve at noon!" Running to the window, he looks out to see if indeed "night had beaten off bright day, and taken possession of the world." Happily, it appears to be midnight in fact, night has not swallowed up day, and time seems still the regular medium in which Scrooge has conducted his business, "a great relief, because 'three days after sight of this First of Exchange pay to Mr. Ebenezer Scrooge or his order,' and so forth, would have become a mere United States' security if there were no days to count by."

Scrooge counts by this time, a concrete fact, hard, impersonal, unyielding, shaped in his own image to badger others in the service of his own prosperity. It is the time of notes and bills, equated with money: so many hours for so much pay, and so many days at so much interest per day. Time, for Scrooge, is money; Bob Cratchit's day off with pay is a double deprivation. "It's not convenient," he complains, "and it's not fair. If I was to stop half-a-crown for it, you'd think yourself ill-used, I'll be bound. . . . And yet . . . you don't think *me* ill-used, when I pay a day's wages for no work." Christmas is merely a "poor excuse for picking a man's pocket every twenty-fifth of December!" Such abstractly quantitative time has no qualities, no seasonal associations: "Out upon merry Christmas! What's Christmas time to you," he expostulates in reply to his nephew's friendly greeting, "but a time for paying bills without money; a time for finding yourself a year older, but not an hour richer; a time for balancing your books and having every item in 'em through a round dozen of months presented dead against you?" Unless one makes money, time is "dead against you."

CIRCULAR TIME

Against this calendrical and quantitative chronology Dickens sets Scrooge's nephew. For him, time has qualities, as well as quantity:

> "I am sure I have always thought of Christmas time, when it has come round—apart from the veneration due to its sacred name and origin, if anything belonging to it can be apart from that—as a good time; a kind, forgiving, charitable, pleasant time; the only time I know of, in the long calendar of the year, when men and women seem by one consent to open their shut-up hearts freely, and to think of people below them as if they really were fellow-passengers to the grave, and not another race of creatures bound on other journeys."

This time is not linear, abstract, discrete, and regularly sequential, not measured by calendars and reliable repeaters and the customary alteration of days and nights, but circular ("when it has come round" contrasts with the linear and computational senses of "a round dozen of months"), recurrent (instead of repetitive), ceremonial, emotional, and, by virtue of the similarity of response called up in all men and women each time, oddly stationary. That is, every Christmas "men and women seem by one consent to open their shut-up hearts freely," and thus every Christmas is to that extent and in that way like every other Christmas. Scrooge's time makes one older, and, he plans, richer; his nephew's makes time almost stand still.

HUMAN TIME

Both speakers refer to a third kind of time, the span of one human life, from birth to death. Scrooge deplores getting older without getting richer; his nephew thinks that Christmas time compensates for the "long calendar of the year," and speaks of the span of human life as a journey "to the grave." We confront finite human time at the beginning of the novel, which is an end: "Marley was dead, to begin with." His passing has been confirmed, in a sense determined, by the signatures in the burial register of the officiating "clergyman, the clerk, the undertaker, and the chief mourner. Scrooge signed it. And Scrooge's name was good upon 'Change for anything he chose to put his hand to." Scrooge knows Marley is dead. And Dickens insists vehemently—if ultimately ironically—upon this fact. "There is no doubt that Marley was dead. This must be distinctly understood, or nothing wonderful can come of the story I am going to relate."

Paradoxically, Marley has not altogether ceased to exist on the face of the earth. Scrooge has gradually turned into Marley, assumed his worldly goods as sole assign and sole residuary legatee, and moved into the "chambers which had once belonged to his deceased partner," and which looked as if they had run to their gloomy location as a playful young house, and "forgotten the way out again," growing old as their inhabitant. His identity is interchangeable with that once belonging to Marley; though he is willing to sign his own name to a burial register, he cannot bring himself to efface his partner's name from the door.

> Scrooge never painted out Old Marley's name. There it stood, years afterwards, above the warehouse door: Scrooge and

Marley. The firm was known as Scrooge and Marley. Sometimes people new to the business called Scrooge Scrooge, and sometimes Marley, but he answered to both names. It was all the same to him.

Moreover, like Marley, Scrooge grows corpselike and metallic. Marley is "as dead as a door-nail." Or a coffin-nail, which the narrator is "inclined . . . to regard . . . as the deadest piece of ironmongery in the trade." Scrooge too is slowly reifying:

> Hard and sharp as flint, from which no steel had ever struck out generous fire; secret, and self-contained, and solitary as an oyster. The cold within him froze his old features, nipped his pointed nose, shrivelled his cheek, stiffened his gait; made his eyes red, his thin lips blue; and spoke out shrewdly in his grating voice.

Cold and solitary, he is unaffected by external heat and cold, as unresponsive to the weather as a corpse. He is likewise unaffected by his "fellow-passengers to the grave," having, in a sense, got there already: no one ever stops him in the street to inquire after his health, or solicit funds, "no children asked him what it was o'clock, no man or woman ever once in all his life inquired the way to such and such a place." He takes delight in warding off all human commerce: "To edge his way along the crowded paths of life, warning all human sympathy to keep its distance, was what the knowing ones call 'nuts' to Scrooge."

TIME AFTER DEATH

If Scrooge is nearly a piece of dead ironmongery, however, Marley is more alive than he, or we, suspect, and first presents himself to his former partner in the guise of a door-knocker, suddenly, "without its undergoing any intermediate process of change," transformed into his face. A fourth kind of time present in the opening stave of the *Carol* is the time after death, the time, adumbrated in Dickens' favorite Scriptural texts, the Gospels and especially the Sermon on the Mount, when the characteristics of this life are reversed. Since Marley was cold and impervious, like Scrooge, and accustomed to such chilly surroundings as Scrooge provides for Bob Cratchit, now his "hair was curiously stirred, as if by breath or hot air," and his "hair, and skirts, and tassels, were still agitated as by the hot vapour from an oven." Since he remained shut up in his counting house during life, and like

Scrooge took no notice or thought of his fellow passengers, he must make his journey now. "It is required of every man," he instructs Scrooge, "that the spirit within him should walk abroad among his fellow-men, and travel far and wide; and if that spirit goes not forth in life, it is condemned to do so after death. It is doomed to wander through the world." Since Marley, again like Scrooge, made the passing hours pay, he is now shackled by the chain he forged in life, a chain clasped about his vacant bowels, made "of cash-boxes, keys, padlocks, ledgers, deeds, and heavy purses wrought in steel." The constipation of his life has taken a dreadful, if appropriate, revenge.

HISTORICAL TIME

A fifth kind of time present in the opening stave of the *Carol* is the historical time of the story. It occurs, apparently, in the present of its first readers' lives. There are sufficient references to familiar and topical affairs and locations—to 'Change, Sabbatarianism, prisons, Union workhouses, Lord Mayor and Mansion House, Joe Miller's jest book, cockney street boys who employ contemporary London slang ("Walk-ER")—to anchor the world to London, circa 1843, for us a clearly defined actual historical past. Indeed, John Butt has traced the topics on Dickens' mind in the months preceding the *Carol*s composition, and shown how many of these subjects appear in his Christmas book. But Dickens calls his tale "a whimsical kind of masque," and immediately after the principal character and situation have been introduced, the story makes a new beginning with the conventional formula for romance or fable or myth: "Once upon a time—of all the good days in the year, on Christmas Eve—old Scrooge sat busy in his counting-house." The *Carol* seems to participate in not just a fictionally historical, but also a fictive, time. This feeling is reinforced by the presence of Ghosts, who, Dickens insists, cannot be dismissed as products of Scrooge's fancy: "Scrooge had as little of what is called fancy about him as any man in the city of London, even including—which is a bold word—the corporation, aldermen, and livery." Nor can they all be ascribed to "a slight disorder of the stomach" that makes Scrooge's senses cheat, no matter how much, to distract his own attention, and keep down his terror, he tries to be waggish and renounce Marley by such feeble verbal fencing: "You may be an undigested bit of beef, a blot of mustard, a crumb of cheese, a fragment of an underdone potato. There's more of gravy than of grave about you, whatever you are!"

Considering the historicity of the temporal setting, if we reject Scrooge's attempt to discredit and disavow their reality, the status of the Ghosts is by no means clear. For one thing, we must distinguish between Marley, literally a *geist,* a spirit, and the three Christmas Phantoms, which are not the immortal remains of individual human lives. For another, we *do* know only through our senses, as Marley reminds Scrooge. In insisting on the analogy between the narrator's voice and the Christmas Ghosts, Dickens provides one way of taking their eruption into the fictional world: our senses respond to his voice as Scrooge does to the Ghosts, and we respond to the story he tells as Scrooge does to the times which the Ghosts present.

A Christmas Carol's Fairy-Tale Format

Harry Stone

> Dickens's Christmas books are essentially fairy tales, writes Harry Stone. In the following excerpt from his book *Dickens and the Invisible World: Fairy Tales, Fantasy, and Novel-Making,* Stone describes how Dickens perfectly executes the fairy-tale technique to shape *A Christmas Carol* and convey its moral lesson. For example, the storybook format allows Dickens to commingle realistic detail with magical happenings, to juxtapose scenes, and to manipulate time. By means of this structure, Dickens clearly and powerfully enforces the tale's moral lesson: that self-interest is harmful and that even a hardened individual like Scrooge can recapture a spirit of childhood and community.

In the interval between the beginning of *Martin Chuzzlewit* and the completion of *Dombey and Son,* Dickens wrote five Christmas books: *A Christmas Carol* (1843), *The Chimes* (1844), *The Cricket on the Hearth* (1845), *The Battle of Life* (1846), and *The Haunted Man* (1848). *The Haunted Man,* the last of the Christmas books, straddles the later limits of this interval. *The Haunted Man* was conceived and partly written in the interval, but not finished until *Dombey* was completed. With the exception of *The Battle of Life,* which depends for its central mechanism on a straightforward analogy between life and an ancient battlefield, the Christmas books rely on fairy-tale machinery to gain their characteristic effects. But this puts the matter too restrictively. The Christmas books draw their innermost energies from fairy tales: they exploit fairy-tale themes, fairy-tale happenings, and fairy-tale techniques. Indeed the Christmas books *are*

Excerpted from *Dickens and the Invisible World: Fairy Tales, Fantasy, and Novel Making,* by Harry Stone (Bloomington: Indiana University Press). Copyright © 1979 by Harry Stone. Reprinted with permission from the author.

fairy tales. As Dickens himself put it, he was here taking old nursery tales and "giving them a higher form."

The pattern that Dickens traces in each of his Christmas books—always excepting *The Battle of Life*—is the pattern that he followed with "Gabriel Grub" in *Pickwick*. The design could hardly be simpler or more direct. A protagonist who is mistaken or displays false values is forced, through a series of extraordinary events, to see his errors. This familiar, almost pedestrian given is interfused with fairy-tale elements, a commingling that shapes and transfigures every aspect of the design. Storybook signs set the mood, herald the onset of the action, and enforce the moral lessons. Magical happenings dominate the story. The crucial action takes place in a dream or vision presided over by supernatural creatures who control what goes on. The resolution occurs when the happenings of the vision—a magically telescoped survey of the protagonist's life, and a masquelike representation of the consequences of his false attitudes—force him to reassess his views. In the fashion of most fairy stories, the moral is strongly reiterated at the end.

This structure was of immense value to Dickens. It gave him a framework that provided an aesthetic justification for the legerdemain which in his earlier works, especially in his finales, had usually appeared, not as fairy-tale felicities, but as arbitrary fairy-tale wrenchings. He could now show misery and horror and yet do so in a context of joyful affirmation. He could depict evil flourishing to its ultimate flowering and still deny that flowering. He could introduce the most disparate scenes, events, and visions without losing the reader's confidence. He could manipulate time with no need to obey the ordinary laws of chronology. He could make his characters and events real when he wished them real, magical when he wished them magical. He could effect overnight conversions which could be justified aesthetically. He could teach by parable rather than exhortation. And he could deal with life in terms of a storybook logic that underscored both the real and the ideal.

A Christmas Carol

These potentialities, fundamental ingredients in Dickens' mature narrative method (but there thoroughly assimilated to the dominant realism), are exploited with varying degrees of success in all the Christmas books. In *A Christmas Carol*, to take the first of the Christmas books, Dickens adapts fairy-tale effects and fairy-tale techniques with marvelous skill. All readers are aware of the ghosts and spirits that manipulate the story, but these supernatural beings are only the most obvious signs of a pervasive indebtedness to fairy stories. Dickens himself emphasized that indebtedness. He subtitled his novelette *A Ghost Story of Christmas,* and he followed this spectral overture with other magical associations. In the preface to the *Carol* he told potential readers that he had endeavored "in this ghostly little book, to raise the Ghost of an Idea." Then he went on: "May it haunt their houses pleasantly and no one wish to lay it!" The chapter headings continue this emphasis. Four of the five headings reinforce supernatural expectations: "Marley's Ghost," "The First of the Three Spirits," "The Second of the Three Spirits," and "The Last of the Spirits." With such signposts at the outset, we can expect the journey itself to be full of wondrous events. We are not disappointed, though the opening begins disarmingly enough. It insists on the deadness of Marley and then drifts into a long, facetious reference to the ghost of Hamlet's father. The narrator's attitude is worldly and commonsensical, but Marley's deadness and the ghost of Hamlet's father set the scene for the wild events that are about to take place.

Scrooge sets the scene too. He has much of the archetypal miser in him, but he is more of an ordinary man than his immediate prototypes, prototypes such as Gabriel Grub, Arthur Gride, Ralph Nickleby, and Jonas Chuzzlewit. Yet at the same time Scrooge is compassed round with supernatural attributes that cunningly suffuse his fundamental realism. One soon sees how this process works. The freezing cold that pervades his inner being frosts all his external features and outward mannerisms (nipped and pointed nose, shrivelled cheek, stiffened gait, red eyes, blue lips, grating voice), and this glacial iciness chills all the world without. "He carried his own low temperature always about with him; he iced his office in the dog-days; and didn't thaw it one degree at Christmas. . . . No warmth could warm, no wintry weather chill him." In this respect Scrooge is a prototype of Mr. Dombey. That cold gentleman freezes and congeals his small universe with haughty frostiness.

The story proper of *A Christmas Carol* begins with the traditional "Once upon a time." After this evocative opening

Dickens quickly intensifies the storybook atmosphere. Scrooge lives in Marley's old chambers, and Marley died seven years ago on Christmas Eve, that is, seven years ago on the night the story opens. It is a foggy night. Nearby houses dwindle mysteriously into "mere phantoms"; ghostly forms loom dimly in the hazy mist. Out of such details, out of cold, fog, and frost, and out of brief touches of contrasting warmth, Dickens builds an atmosphere dense with personification, animism, anthropomorphism, and the like. The inanimate world is alive and active; every structure, every object plays its percipient role in the unfolding drama. Buildings and gateways, bedposts and door knockers become sentient beings that conspire in a universal morality. Everything is connected by magical means to everything else. Scrooge's chambers are a case in point. The narrator tells us that they are in a lonely, isolated building that must have played hide-and-seek with other houses in its youth, run into a yard where it had no business to be, forgotten its way out again, and remained there ever since. This lost, isolated, cutoff building, fit residence for a lost, isolated, cutoff man, has its own special weather and tutelary spirit. The fog and frost hang so heavy about the black old gateway of this building "that it seemed as if the Genius of the Weather sat in mournful meditation on the threshold."

MARLEY'S GHOST

Given a universe so magical and responsive, we are hardly surprised when Scrooge momentarily sees Marley's face glowing faintly in his front-door knocker, its "ghostly spectacles turned up on its ghostly forehead." When Scrooge sees an equally ghostly hearse on his staircase a few moments later, we know that he is in for a night of it. Thus we are fully prepared for Marley's ghost when it does appear, and we know how to interpret its every movement and accoutrement. Marley's ghost is a superb compound of social symbolism, wild imagination, realistic detail, and grisly humor. It moves in its own strange atmosphere, its hair and clothes stirring curiously, as though agitated by "the hot vapour from an oven"; it wears a bandage round its head, and when it removes this death cloth, its lower jaw drops down upon its breast. Like Blake's city-pent Londoner, Marley's ghost drags and clanks its "mind-forg'd manacles," the chain it "forged in life" and girded on of its "own free will"; like the ghost of Hamlet's father, it is doomed to walk the night and wander restlessly abroad. Scrooge is skeptical of this apparition, but he is no match for the ghost's supernatural power. Like the Ancient Mariner with the wedding guest, the ghost "hath his will." When Scrooge offers his last resistance, the ghost raises a frightful cry, shakes its chains appallingly, and takes the bandage from round its head. Scrooge falls on his knees and submits. Like the wedding guest, now Scrooge "cannot choose but hear." And as in the *Ancient Mariner,* where the wedding guest's struggle and reluctant submission help us suspend our disbelief, in *A Christmas Carol* Scrooge's struggle and submission help us to a like suspension. The ghost has accomplished its mission; the work of the three spirits, work that will culminate in Scrooge's redemption (and our enlightenment), can now begin.

THE THREE SPIRITS

The three spirits or ghosts (Dickens uses the terms interchangeably) are allegorical figures as well as supernatural agents. The Ghost of Christmas Past combines in his person and in his actions distance and closeness, childhood and age, forgetfulness and memory; in a similar fashion the Ghost of Christmas Present is a figure of ease, plenty, and joy—an embodiment of the meaning of Christmas; the Ghost of Christmas Yet to Come, on the other hand, a hooded and shrouded Death, bears implacable witness to the fatal course Scrooge has been pursuing. Each spirit, in other words, enacts a role and presides over scenes that befit its representation. But it is the scenes rather than the spirits that are all-important. The scenes embody Dickens' message in swift vignettes and unforgettable paradigms—Fezziwig's ball, the Cratchits' Christmas dinner, Scrooge's lonely grave. By means of the fairy-tale machinery Dickens can move instantaneously from magic-lantern picture to magic-lantern picture, juxtaposing, contrasting, commenting, and counterpointing, and he can do all this with absolute freedom and ease. He can evoke the crucial image, limn the archetypal scene, concentrate on the traumatic spot of time, with no need to sketch the valleys in between. Like Le Sage much earlier in *The Devil upon Two Sticks* (a boyhood favorite of Dickens), he can fly over the unsuspecting city, lift its imperturbable rooftops, and reveal swift tableaus of pathos and passion; like Joyce much later in the opening pages of *A Portrait of the Artist as a Young Man,* he can race through the years, linger here and there, and provide brief glimpses of the unregarded moments that move and shape us. The overall effect, however, is more like that of a richly colored Japanese screen. Amid swirling mists and dense clouds one glimpses prototypical scenes of serenity and turmoil, joy and nightmare horror.

Through Scrooge Dickens attempts to embody symbolic, social, psychological, and mythic truth. Scrooge is an outrageous miser and ogre, but he is also an emblem of more ordinary pathology: he is an epitome of all selfish and self-regarding men. In his latter aspect, he touches our lives. He allows us to see how self-interest—an impulse that motivates each one of us—can swell to monster proportions. He shows us how not to live, and then, at the end, he points us toward salvation. That lesson has social as well as symbolic ramifications. We are made to see that in grinding Bob Cratchit Scrooge grinds himself, that in letting Tiny Tim perish he perishes alive himself. All society is connected: individual actions are not self-contained and personal, they have social consequences; social evils are not limited and discrete, they taint the whole society. These ideas, of course, were not unique to Dickens. They were being preached by many Victorians, by two such different men—both friends of Dickens—as Douglas Jerrold and Thomas Carlyle, for example. But Dickens presents these ideas in a more seductive guise than any of his contemporaries. And he blends teaching with much else.

CHILDHOOD WOUNDS

For one thing, he merges symbolic paradigms and social doctrines with psychological analysis. By means of a few swift childhood vignettes he gives us some notion of why Scrooge became what he is. The first spirit shows Scrooge an image of his early self: "a solitary child, neglected by his friends," and left alone in school at Christmas time. This scene of loneliness and neglect is mitigated by a single relief: the boy's intense reading. The reading is not simply referred to, it comes to life, a bright pageant of color and warmth in his drab isolation. The exotic characters from that reading troop into the barren room and enact their familiar adventures. Scenes from *The Arabian Nights* flash before Scrooge, then images from *Valentine and Orson,* then vignettes from *The Arabian Nights* again, then episodes from *Robinson Crusoe*—all as of yore, all wonderfully thrilling and absorbing. Scrooge is beside himself with excitement. The long-forgotten memory of his lonely self and of his succoring reading softens him: he remembers what it was to be a child; he wishes that he had given something to the boy who sang a Christmas carol at his door the night before. A moment later Scrooge is looking at a somewhat older image of his former self, again alone in a school, again left behind at Christmas time. But now his

---

ICONOGRAPHIC SCENES

As Paul Davis notes, most readers remember A Christmas Carol *as a cluster of specific phrases and images that transcend a purely textual account of Scrooge's life.*

As a ritual of cyclic retelling, the *Carol* is, as [Dickens critic Stephen] Leacock points out, "better known in scenes, . . . than at its full length." We recognize Scrooge in his office with Cratchit in his cell, without being told that it is a scene from Dickens' story, and the image of Bob Cratchit holding Tiny Tim on his shoulder has become so indelibly fixed in our imagination that we can identify it in silhouette. The iconographic method pictorializes the story, turning it from continuous narrative into a chain of remembered scenes, a series of visual stations along its narrative journey. This visual version of the *Carol* represents Dickens' sense of Christmas. . . .

We know Scrooge's life as a set of images: bent over his desk in the cold office, denying coal to his clerk; standing in amazement before his door knocker; kneeling in fright before Marley's ghost. We see him as a child reading in a lonely schoolroom; as a young man preparing the warehouse for Fezziwig's party; as an old man cowering before his gravestone; as a reformed man leaning out his window on Christmas morning and asking the boy in the street what day it is. This magic-lantern technique piles all the Christmases in Scrooge's life one on top of the other and allows for rapid transitions in the narrative, creating a visual shorthand to tell the essentials of Scrooge's life. It also connects our consciousness with those of the narrator and Scrooge, for we understand Scrooge's life as he does, as spots of time in his consciousness of his own personal history. The rapid transitions from one of these moments to the next embody in microcosm the principle of conversion at the core of the story.

Paul Davis, *The Lives and Times of Ebenezer Scrooge.* New Haven, CT: Yale University Press, 1990.

sister Fan enters and tells him that he can come home at last, that father is kinder now and will permit him to return, that Scrooge is to be a man and "never to come back here" again. These memories also soften Scrooge.

The memories, of course, are versions of Dickens' own experiences: the lonely boy "reading as if for life," and saved by that reading; the abandoned child, left in Chatham to finish the Christmas term, while the family goes off to London; the banished son (banished while Fanny remains free), exiled by his father to the blacking warehouse and then released by him at last. These wounding experiences, or rather the *Carol* version of them, help turn Scrooge (and here he is very different from the outward Dickens) into a lonely, isolated man intent on insulating himself from harm or hurt. In a subsequent vignette, a vignette between him and his fiancée, Scrooge chooses money over love. He is the victim of his earlier wound. He seeks through power and aggrandizement to gird himself against the vulnerability that had scarred his childhood. But in making himself invulnerable, he shuts out humanity as well. This happens to Scrooge because, paradoxically, in trying to triumph over his past, he has forgotten it; he has forgotten what it is to be a child, he has forgotten what it is to be lonely and friendless, to cry, laugh, imagine, yearn, and love. The first spirit, through memory, helps Scrooge recover his past, helps him recover the humanness (the responsiveness and fellow feeling) and the imagination (the reading and the visions) that were his birthright, that are every man's birthright.

All this, and much more, is done swiftly and economically with the aid of Dickens' fairy-tale format. The rapid shifts from scene to scene, the spirits' pointed questions and answers, the telescoping, blurring, and juxtaposition of time, the fusion of allegory, realism, psychology, and fancy—all are made possible, all are brought into order and believability, by Dickens' storybook atmosphere and storybook devices. *A Christmas Carol* has a greater unity of effect, a greater concentration of thematic purpose, a greater economy of means towards ends, and a greater sense of integration and cohesiveness than any previous work by Dickens.

SCROOGE: A UNIVERSAL EMBLEM

A Christmas Carol is the finest of the Christmas books. This preeminence results from its consummate melding of the most archetypal losses, fears, and yearnings with the most lucid embodiment of such elements in characters and actions. No other Christmas book displays this perfect coming together of concept and vehicle. The result is a most powerful, almost mythic statement of widely held truths and aspirations. Scrooge represents every man who has hardened his heart, lost his ability to feel, separated himself from his fellow men, or sacrificed his life to ego, power, or accumulation. The symbolic force of Scrooge's conversion is allied to the relief we feel (since we are all Scrooges, in part) in knowing that we too can change and be reborn. This is why we are moved by the reborn Scrooge's childlike exultation in his prosaic physical surroundings, by his glee at still having time to give and share. We too can exult in "Golden sunlight; Heavenly sky; sweet fresh air; merry bells"; we too can cry, "Oh, glorious. Glorious!"; we too can give and share. Scrooge assures us that we can advance from the prison of self to the paradise of community. The *Carol's* fairy-tale structure helps in that assurance. The structure evokes and objectifies the undefiled world of childhood and makes us feel that we, like Scrooge, can recapture it. Deep symbolic identifications such as these, identifications that stir us whether we are consciously aware of them or not, give *A Christmas Carol* its enduring grip on our culture. *A Christmas Carol* is a myth or fairy tale for our times, one that is still full of life and relevance. Its yearly resurrection in advertisement, cartoon, and television program, its reappearance in new versions (in Bergman's *Wild Strawberries,* to cite only one instance), testify to this.

Yet the vitality of *A Christmas Carol* raises other questions. Why is the *Carol,* which elaborates the central idea found in the Gabriel Grub story in *Pickwick,* so much better than its prototype? "Gabriel Grub" does not elicit the empathy of the *Carol.* This is so because Gabriel never ascends to universality; he is simply a mean man who is taught an idiosyncratic lesson. We see nothing of his childhood, of his development, of his future; we see nothing, in other words, of the shaping forces that would allow us to relate to his experiences. The story centers on his drunken vision; it scants his salvation and our enlightenment. Furthermore, "Gabriel Grub" lacks any rich social import. Unlike the *Carol,* there is virtually no intertwining of plot with social criticism: no ideas about ignorance and want, no anatomy of materialism, no criticism of relations between employer and employee, no effective demonstration of how to live. Misanthropy is simply presented and then punished. I am not suggesting that a work of art must have a social message. I am simply affirming that part of the *Carol*'s appeal comes from its powerful demonstration of how a man should live—live in society—if he is to save his soul, a kind of demonstration that is largely lacking in "Gabriel Grub."

By the same token, the supernatural machinery of "Gabriel Grub," despite successful local effects, is mechanical and abrupt. Unlike the *Carol*, where Marley's ghost is the culmination of many signs and actions, in "Gabriel Grub" the King of the Goblins appears with little preparation; again, unlike the *Carol*, where Marley's ghost is a prototype of Scrooge, and therefore deeply significant, in "Gabriel Grub" the King of the Goblins is simply an agency, a convenient manipulative device, a creature who has no relevance to Gabriel's life and habits (other, perhaps, than being an emanation of Gabriel's habitual drunkenness). Even the *Carol* equivalents to the King of the Goblins, the three spirits, have an allegorical pertinence that the King of the Goblins lacks. In part these differences in the two stories are owing to differences in length, but more importantly they are owing to differences in conception and execution. Obviously the preeminence of the *Carol*, its elevation to culture fable, comes not from the basic ingredients—they can be found in "Gabriel Grub"—but from the perfect blending of well-wrought theme and well-wrought form. *A Christmas Carol* demonstrates how much more skilled Dickens had become in using fairy-tale conceptions to achieve that virtuoso blending, how adept he had become in using fairy-tale elements to integrate and convey his view of life.

The Character
of the Narrator

James A. Davies

The narrator is a strong character in *A Christmas Carol*, writes James A. Davies. In the following essay, Davies describes the limits of a textual account of Scrooge's life and critiques the *Carol*'s narrator, including how the narrator reveals his character and shapes the work. Davies concludes that the paternalistic narrator is somewhat callous, patronizing, emotionally withdrawn, and sexually repressed. Davies is the author of *The Textual Life of Dickens's Characters,* from which the following critical analysis is excerpted.

The concept of the fictional-work-as-monologue is . . . central to understanding *A Christmas Carol* but my discussion of the tale begins with the famous illustrations and their relationship to the text. This link is not a simple one, for though some pictures, such as the opening embodiment of benevolent paternalism in 'Mr Fezziwig's Ball', the chained phantoms sharing Marley's fate, or Scrooge attempting to extinguish the light of Christmas Past, are simple visual renderings of textual points, others are not. For example, the Scrooge of the text is 'a squeezing, wrenching, grasping, scraping, clutching, covetous old sinner! Hard and sharp as flint. . . . The cold within him froze his old features, nipped his pointed nose, shrivelled his cheek, stiffened his gait . . .'. This is not the person seen in 'Marley's Ghost', nor in 'Scrooge's third Visitor'. The Scrooge we see there is old, vulnerable and full of amiable curiosity. In 'Scrooge's third Visitor', he is fascinated and attracted by the vibrant presence of the Ghost and the food and drink heaped around him. Further, in the plate of 'Marley's Ghost' the colours are unexpected. Scrooge's living-room, described in the text as part of a 'gloomy suite of rooms', glows, in the illustration, with rich purple, blue, yellow and brown, the colours of life and growth. The foot-stool waits to enable a more indulgent Scrooge to escape the draught. The two illustrations suggest the human potential, the latent goodness, in both the man and his surroundings.

Stave III ends with Scrooge's confrontation with Ignorance and Want, arguably the most powerful and moving part of the text:

> From the foldings of its robe, it brought two children; wretched, abject, frightful, hideous, miserable. They knelt down at its feet, and clung upon the outside of its garment.
>
> 'Oh, Man! look here. Look, look, down here!' exclaimed the Ghost.
>
> They were a boy and girl. Yellow, meagre, ragged, scowling, wolfish; but prostrate, too, in their humility. Where graceful youth should have filled their features out, and touched them with its freshest tints, a stale and shrivelled hand, like that of age, had pinched, and twisted them, and pulled them into shreds. Where angels might have sat enthroned, devils lurked; and glared out menacing. No change, no degradation, no perversion of humanity, in any grade, through all the mysteries of wonderful creation, has monsters half so horrible and dread. . . .
>
> 'Spirit! are they yours?' Scrooge could say no more.
>
> 'They are Man's,' said the Spirit, looking down upon them. 'And they cling to me, appealing from their fathers. This boy is Ignorance. This girl is Want. Beware them both, and all of their degree, but most of all beware this boy, for on his brow I see that written which is Doom, unless the writing be erased. Deny it!' cried the Spirit, stretching out its hand towards the city. 'Slander those who tell it ye! Admit it for your factious purposes, and make it worse. And bide the end!'

The Spirit, in referring to Scrooge as 'Man' and the children as 'Man's' and in 'stretching out its hand towards the city' suggests that the existence of ignorance and want is the fault of Scrooge and those like him, wealthy individuals whose money is not put to proper use. The scene, like the story, is an argument for benevolent paternalism. But in the illustration the confrontation takes place against a background of Victorian factory-buildings with their smoking stacks. The point is a different one: the 'yellow, meagre, ragged, scowling, wolfish' children of the text, the existence of ignorance and want, are the dreadful products of unrestrained industrialism, of which the nineteenth-century factory system, in particular its use of child labour, is a dreadful manifestation.

The book's final pages are much concerned with the changed relationship between the converted Scrooge and Bob Cratchit, the jovial boss assuring his astonished clerk, 'I'll raise your salary, and endeavour to assist your struggling family, and we will discuss your affairs this very afternoon, over a Christmas bowl of smoking bishop'. On the venue for that discussion the text is silent but the final illustration shows Scrooge, foot comfortably on foot-stool, in his seasonally decorated living-room, ladling out punch for an eager Bob. The text asserts improved working relationships between master and man, the illustration socialising, benevolent to the extent that the worker is invited to the boss's home. That said, the illustration makes Bob childlike: his feet hardly touch the floor, his umbrella is as long as he is, Scrooge is fatherly towards him. Paternalism remains the keynote and the picture extends its scope.

THE NARRATOR'S LIMITATIONS

The illustrations, then, are an integral part of *A Christmas Carol*. They expose the limitations of the purely textual exploration of Scrooge's characterisation and Victorian social ills. In that the illustrations and text *combined* exhibit the complete work's wide-ranging insight into social conditions, the text alone necessarily indicates the Narrator's limitations. His is not the complete picture.

The story's opening is well-known:

> Marley was dead: to begin with. There is no doubt whatever about that. . . . Old Marley was as dead as a door-nail.

> Mind! I don't mean to say that I know, of my own knowledge, what there is particularly dead about a door-nail. . . .

The bluff, insistent, buttonholing manner reminds us of similar openings but in a different *genre:*

> No more wine? then we'll push back chairs and talk. A final glass for me, though . . .

or

> I am poor brother Lippo, by your leave!
> You need not clap your torches to my face.

or

> You know, we French stormed Ratisbon:
> A mile or so away . . .

These lines from, respectively, 'Bishop Blougram's Apology', 'Fra Lippo Lippi', and 'Incident of the French Camp', remind us that the age of Dickens was also that of Robert Browning and that the dramatic monologue was a ubiquitous form that has been precisely described:

> [It] should include a first-person speaker who is not the poet and whose character is unwittingly revealed, an auditor whose influence is felt in the poem, a specific time and place, colloquial language, some sympathetic involvement with the speaker, and an ironic discrepancy between the speaker's view of himself and a larger judgment which the poet implies and the reader must develop.

The relevance of this definition to a prose work like *A Christmas Carol* is immediately apparent. Indeed, Dickens himself realised his tale's monologising qualities: *A Christmas Carol* was a natural choice for the first public reading that he gave and, during the reading tours, the one he usually chose for important performances. This discussion will return to notions of sympathy and ironic discrepancy; here, the palpable presence of an auditor can first be stressed. He is, for instance, the person to whose queries the Narrator responds: 'Scrooge knew he was dead?' echoes the latter, 'Of course he did. How could it be otherwise?'. In Stave II the Narrator observes that Scrooge was as close to the Ghost of Christmas Past 'as I am now to you, and I am standing in the spirit at your elbow', the moment above all others in which the Narrator's as well as the listener/reader's separate characterisation can be clearly discerned.

NARRATOR VERSUS AUTHOR

So far as the Narrator's characterisation is concerned very few critics have much to say. Indeed, some famous discussions of the tale fail to make any proper distinction between Narrator and Author. Chesterton, for example, though noting that the tale's 'festive and popular' style counters ostensibly bleak events and scenes, thus implicitly recognising the importance of narrative tone, assumes the style to be Dickens's own and leaves it at that. Edgar Johnson, in his influential study of Scrooge as 'the personification of "economic man"', also makes no distinction between Narrator and Author.

Later, more critically-aware analyses include Deborah Thomas on the relevance of the dramatic monologue term to many of Dickens's short pieces and his use of the 'first-person narrative as a tool for revealing mental processes'. Michael Slater argues shrewdly that, in *A Christmas Carol* we receive 'an overwhelming impression of the story-teller's physical proximity' and the story-teller is understood as 'a jolly, kind-hearted bachelor uncle', generally joking and festive, occasionally sharp about the state of the country, momentarily grim in Stave III, when treating Scrooge's confrontation with Ignorance and Want. Graham Holderness, in a perceptive interpretation of the tale as Scrooge's rejection of materialism and cultivation of the sympathetic imagination, includes an important discussion of the Narrator's character. He argues that the Narrator embodies 'the power of imagination', expressed via the qualities of 'energy and vitality, humour and imagination' so evident in most of the narrative, that eventually shapes and educates Scrooge. Holderness, though, is forced to conclude that, because we are so impressed by the Narrator's qualities, the final section of the tale disappoints: the prose loses its imaginative life and the Narrator declines into a sentimental conclusion.

Slater and Holderness can be persuasive. Both regard the Narrator as a positive and essentially simple character. Yet even the tale's opening suggests the inadequacy of these views. The narrative persona is hearty and emphatic, the bachelor uncle of Slater's account, but that it is also oddly self-conscious and insecure is evident in the way he scrutinises his own clichés: the statement that 'Old Marley was as dead as a door-nail' is followed by a paragraph discussing the appropriateness of the image. In the dismissive comment that ends that discussion—'But the wisdom of our ancestors is in the simile, and my unhallowed hands shall not disturb it, or the country's done for'—is a jocular but contemptuous view of popular sentiment. Behind the heartiness is a defensively prickly personality.

Through the opening pages this defensiveness is evident in three aspects of the narrative. First, the insistence on its fictiveness, effected mainly through obvious patterning that emphasises the Narrator as maker as well as teller. We see this in a small way as Marley's Ghost departs: 'at every step it took, the window raised itself a little'. The scene is manifestly contrived, here to retain distancing humour. More centrally, as a number of critics have pointed out, there is an enhanced concern for form and structure seen in the tale's precise divisions, and careful linking of parts evident, for example, in Scrooge's remarks on prisons and death being thrown back at him by the second spirit, in the philanthropic gentlemen in Stave I reappearing in the final stave to show Scrooge's new attitudes, in the careful contrasting of the chronological progression of the Spirit-scenes with the tale's timeless present, and the equally careful concern not only with the course of Scrooge's life but with its consequences. Small, early details have the same effect: the reader, insists the Narrator, must understand that Marley was dead, otherwise 'nothing wonderful can come of the story I am going to relate'. Having emphasised the importance of fictional conventions he begins the action proper with a deliberate 'Once upon a time'.

Second, a development of the first, is the Narrator's over-insistence on the facts, evident throughout and obvious even in the first two sentences: 'Marley was dead: to begin with. There is no doubt whatever about that.' That the Narrator too often protests too much counters any initial sense of this power through knowledge.

Emotional Distance

Third, the Narrator distances himself from the tale's events, and refuses to empathise. This he achieves by undermining seriousness. The first description of Scrooge is deprived of much of its force by its own verve and energy—'Oh! but he was a tight-fisted hand at the grindstone, Scrooge! a squeezing, wrenching, grasping, scraping, clutching, covetous old sinner!'—and by its jokey references to the weather. London fog seems less cold, bleak and polluted, indeed, can seem almost attractive when compared to steam from brewers' chimneys. In the scenes between Scrooge and his nephew, and Scrooge and the philanthropic gentlemen, even though Scrooge's superb diatribes attract us and have more life and force than the sincere platitudes of his visitors, his emotional force is partly neutralised by the way even the dialogue is imbued with some humour: 'At the ominous word "liberality", Scrooge frowned, and shook his head' and

> ' "You wish to be anonymous?"
> "I wish to be left alone," said Scrooge.'

Even one of the tale's serious concerns, the existence of free will, of moral choice, implicit in Marley informing Scrooge that the latter continues to labour on the chain that still frustrates him, is not free from facetiousness: following Marley's words 'Scrooge glanced about him on the floor, in the expectation of finding himself surrounded by some fifty or sixty fathoms of iron cable: but he could see nothing'. The shocking attitudes towards the poor and unfortunate (' "If they would rather die," said Scrooge, "they had better do it, and decrease the surplus population' " become less so when Scrooge's delight in his own repartee allows us to be amused: '[he] resumed his labours with an improved opinion of himself, and in a more facetious temper than was usual with him'. Even in the grimmest passage, the encounter with Ignorance and Want, when the Narrator himself is moved by the youthful apparitions, his treatment of Scrooge hardly maximises pathos: 'Scrooge started back, appalled. Having them shown to him in this way, he tried to say they were fine children, but the words choked themselves, rather than be parties to a lie of such enormous magnitude'. The personifying of 'words' allows a hint of facetiousness even into this dark passage.

Humour is rarely absent from the text; its often fanciful presence, whether in the chattering teeth of a chiming clock, the 'misanthropic ice', Scrooge's house when young 'playing at hide-and-seek with other houses', the knocker in the shape of Marley's face glowing 'like a bad lobster in a dark cellar', prevents full emotional involvement on the Narrator's part as well as on the reader's and mitigates the salutary effect of Scrooge's character and circumstances. All becomes, as the Narrator writes of poulterers and grocers, 'a splendid joke: a glorious pageant'.

These short phrases are examples of a further distancing effect, the use of the formally archaic, at times humorously effective language that increasingly replaces the heartily colloquial. For example: when the Ghost of Christmas Past materialises, the Narrator comments that because of its dissolving tendency 'no outline would be visible in the dense gloom wherein they melted away'. When Scrooge asks the Ghost to cover himself and is reprimanded, he

reverently disclaimed all intention to offend. . . . He then made bold to inquire what business brought him there. . . .

'Rise! and walk with me!'

It would have been in vain for Scrooge to plead that the weather and the hour were not adapted to pedestrian purposes. . . .

During the remainder of the tale the Narrator often escapes from pleasurable engagement or emotional involvement into this highly-formal style. Two examples must suffice: neighbours shovelling snow hurl 'a facetious snowball—better-natured missile far than many a wordy jest', the Ghost takes him through the city 'until besought by Scrooge to tarry for a moment'. The language mocks rather than dignifies; the narrative stance is one of patronising superiority. Certainly the readiness of the humour and the mock-elevation of the style suggest callousness. This last quality, always lurking, on occasion becomes troublingly overt.

To put this another way: the Narrator is all too willing to substitute for humane involvement a *bonhomie* that on occasion can be brutal:

Foggier yet, and colder! Piercing, searching, biting cold. If the good Saint Dunstan had but nipped the Evil Spirit's nose with a touch of such weather as that, instead of using his familiar weapons, then indeed he would have roared to lusty purpose. The owner of one scant young nose, gnawed and mumbled by the hungry cold as bones are gnawed by dogs, stooped down at Scrooge's keyhole to regale him with a Christmas carol: but at the first sound . . . Scrooge seized the ruler with such energy of action, that the singer fled in terror. . . .

The boisterous reference to Saint Dunstan who, in the legend, wielded red-hot pincers, in itself shows a cheerful delight in cruelty. The casual appearance in such a hearty paragraph of the savage simile describing the young carol-singer's nose betrays a disturbing lack of persisting compassion. Equally distasteful and cruel is the sketch of 'a red-faced gentleman with a pendulous excrescence on the end of his nose, that shook like the gills of a turkey-cock'. Such Swiftean fascination for the gross physical attribute is not indicative of warm fellow-feeling.

Pedantic Superiority

A lack of the latter is particularly evident in the treatment of the Cratchits. Bob, the family-man with scanty means and awesome responsibilities, is treated as a child who cheers simple Christmas sentiments, slides with the children, runs home 'as hard as he could pelt, to play at blindman's-buff', and is too often described as 'Little Bob'. During Christmas dinner the family is patronised pedantically: the Narrator pokes fun at their pretence that the small pudding is sufficient and, when they draw around the hearth, corrects Bob's reference to the family 'circle, meaning half a one'. Revealingly, when the Ghost of Christmas Present stops to bless the Cratchits' home, 'Think of that!' cries the Narrator,

> Bob had but fifteen 'Bob' a-week himself; he pocketed on Saturdays but fifteen copies of his Christian name; and yet the Ghost of Christmas Present blessed his four-roomed house!

In insisting that a man's income should not determine his just deserts he succeeds only in implying that it should.

As for the Cratchits' observance of Christmas: along with the knowingness and assumptions of pedantic superiority, the Narrator purveys the belief that even such a poor and unfortunate family can put out of its collective mind all but ideas of happiness and charity, to demonstrate that no circumstance, however hostile, can corrupt their innate Christian feelings. Further, their social compliance—admiration of the aristocracy, satisfaction that son will follow father into penury through clerking, absence of concern for domestic deficiencies—beggars belief as well as themselves. In stating that such a family is 'happy, grateful, pleased with one another, and contented with the time' the Narrator withdraws from considered sympathy with decent but badly-treated folk into sentimental evasion.

Most disturbing of all is his treatment of Tiny Tim's death. A chair is set next to the child's body in the Cratchit bedroom:

> Poor Bob sat down in it, and when he had thought a little and composed himself, he kissed the little face. He was reconciled to what had happened, and went down again quite happy.

The final sentence is breath-taking in its evasive manipulation in the interests of narratorial wish-fulfilment.

REPRESSED SEXUALITY

To the treatment of the Cratchits can be added another troubling and unexpected tendency: as the Ghost of Christmas Past leads Scrooge back through time, his 'grasp, though gentle as a woman's hand, was not to be resisted'. The simile is a small first indication of the Narrator's pronounced sensuality, evident again in his knowing excitement at the dancing at Fezziwig's and, particularly, as Scrooge and the

Ghost observe Scrooge's nephew's family in their drawing-room on Christmas Eve. At first they watch the children play, before the nephew's beautiful young daughter

> soon beginning to mingle in the sports, got pillaged by the young brigands most ruthlessly. What would I not have given to be one of them! Though I never could have been so rude, no, no! I wouldn't for the wealth of all the world have crushed that braided hair, and torn it down; and for the precious little shoe, I wouldn't have plucked it off, God bless my soul! to save my life. As to measuring her waist in sport, as they did, bold young brood, I couldn't have done it; I should have expected my arm to have grown round it for a punishment, and never come straight again. And yet I should have dearly liked, I own, to have touched her lips; to have questioned her, that she might have opened them; to have looked upon the lashes of her downcast eyes, and never raised a blush; to have let loose waves of hair, an inch of which would be a keepsake beyond price: in short, I should have liked, I do confess, to have had the lightest licence of a child, and yet been man enough to know its value.

The passage is intriguing and disturbing in that the imagery of violence first applied to the children's innocent play is then used to express the narrator's feelings for the beautiful daughter. She is regarded as a gratifying object to be tousled, partially stripped and then fondled; the irony and indirection—the cutting of hair suggesting violation—may betray the Narrator's unease and cannot hide his repressed sexuality. Such feelings recur briefly as he describes Christmas festivities observed by Scrooge and the Ghost of Christmas Present, in particular a 'group of handsome girls' visiting a neighbour's house 'where, woe upon the single man who saw them enter—artful witches: well they knew it—in a glow!' and, importantly, in a later scene in the nephew's home. Now, the Narrator drools over Scrooge's niece—

> a dimpled, surprised-looking, capital face; a ripe little mouth, that seemed made to be kissed—as no doubt it was; all kinds of good little dots about her chin, that melted into one another when she laughed; and the sunniest pair of eyes you ever saw in any little creature's head. Altogether she was what you would have called provoking, you know; but satisfactory too. Oh, perfectly satisfactory!

—and savours, in Sternean fashion, Topper's performance at blind-man's buff, his mock-attempts to identify the plump sister by touching her headdress, ring and necklace. Topper's behaviour was 'vile, monstrous! No doubt she told him her opinion of it, when, another blind-man being in office, they were so very confidential together, behind the curtain'. The Narrator assumes a none-too-convincing knowledge of women that serves only to remind us of his presumed bachelor status and repressed sexuality.

The characterising of the Narrator is superbly consistent. His readiness to withdraw from humane involvement, his patronising superiority, make for an uneasy and imperceptive account of Scrooge's career. His inability properly to empathise prevents him from regarding those who feature in his tale as complex human beings deserving consideration for what they actually are. Instead, too many of the characters—the Cratchits, the nephew's family—are manipulated into patterns of wish-fulfilment that include, so far as the latter are concerned, sensual-sexual fantasising.

Thus unlike Holderness, we should not be disappointed at the tale's ending. For Stave V describes a radical and fundamental change of character: the miser becomes the philanthropist. Stave V shows Scrooge expressing the latent benevolence and kindliness of the illustrations. But whereas, in the pictures, the point has positive force, in the text the effect is the opposite. This can be explained by reference to the language. The Narrator regains the heartiness and facetiousness of the tale's opening pages and takes them to the edges of hysteria. Thus, of Scrooge's laugh:

> Really, for a man who had been out of practice for so many years, it was a splendid laugh, a most illustrious laugh. The father of a long, long line of brilliant laughs!

and

> Running to the window, he opened it, and put out his head. No fog, no mist; clear, bright, jovial, stirring, cold; cold, piping for the blood to dance to; Golden sunlight; Heavenly sky; sweet fresh air; merry bells. Oh, glorious. Glorious!

The sense of strain is evident, as is the poverty of a language that seeks effects through exclamatory insistence. Whereas the illustrations contribute to a sense of man's innate goodness, Stave V illustrates the narrator's sentimentality evident in the imposition of a happy ending. Such manipulation and wish-fulfilment are exactly as expected.

To return to Holderness's criticisms of this last section: '[Dickens's] vision of a transformed life is far weaker, far narrower, far less *imaginative*, than his understanding of the world that needs to be transformed' and the resorting to 'abstract virtue', the 'thinness' of which 'can be measured by the unsureness of the prose', means that the story ends with a 'weary, unenthusiastic affirmation of "goodness"'. The trouble with this statement, we now see, is that Holderness neglects the distinction between Author and Narrator. Once that distinction is made and the Narrator's character properly understood, Stave V has to be read differently as, on Dickens's part, a deliberately sentimental effusion proceeding from the Narrator's reactionary, because optimistically paternalistic, viewpoint. We can agree with Holderness that the final section demonstrates the Narrator's grave lack of a sympathetic imagination whilst recognising, as he does not, that this is the tale's essential point.

The Narrator is strongly characterised in all Dickens's writings. In this sense they are all monologues. *A Christmas Carol,* in particular, is properly understood only if it is recognised as such. As has been seen, the illustrations expose the limitations of the monologist's moral and imaginative insight into Scrooge's life and conversion. But whereas the pictures might be said to have a positively deconstructive effect on the text, the force of the Narrator's textual life, asserting his faulty vision, is a substantial subversion of the whole work's attempt at the optimistic gesture that offers understanding as a prelude to effective social action. The Narrator's misconceived and misdirected force and textual life put optimism firmly in its place.

CHAPTER 2

Themes in *A Christmas Carol*

READINGS ON
A CHRISTMAS CAROL

A Christmas Carol and the Search for Lost Innocence

Elliot L. Gilbert

According to Elliot L. Gilbert, *A Christmas Carol* is a metaphysical study of an individual's quest for lost innocence. Gilbert defines metaphysical innocence as immutable and profoundly antirational, describing life as a cyclical journey that moves away from, and then returns to, a state of innocence. It is on this level, writes Gilbert, that Scrooge's conversion derives its conviction: Scrooge's life of frenzied acquisition and miserliness—and his subsequent change of heart—are passionate attempts to reestablish the innocence and wholeness lost in infancy. Gilbert contributed the following critical essay to *PMLA*.

It is impossible to get into a serious discussion of Charles Dickens' *A Christmas Carol* without sooner or later having to confront "the Scrooge problem." Edmund Wilson stated that problem succinctly and dramatically in his well-known essay "The Two Scrooges" when he wrote:

> Shall we ask what Scrooge would actually be like if we were to follow him beyond the frame of the story? Unquestionably, he would relapse, when the merriment was over—if not while it was still going on—into moroseness, vindictiveness, suspicion. He would, that is to say, reveal himself as the victim of a manic-depressive cycle, and a very uncomfortable person.

Other critics have made much the same point about Scrooge. Humphry House, for example, remarked about the old man's conversion that

> it seems to be complete at a stroke, his actions after it uniform. There is no hint of his needing at intervals to recruit his

Excerpted from "The Ceremony of Innocence: Charles Dickens's *A Christmas Carol*," by Elliot L. Gilbert, *PMLA*, January 1975. Reprinted with permission from Modern Language Association of America; © 1975 (endnotes in the original have been omitted in this reprint).

strength for the new part he has to play; there are implied no periods of restlessness or despondency.

Biographer Edgar Johnson, briefly summarizing this critical approach to *A Christmas Carol,* added his own speculation about how such an attitude might have developed. "There have been readers," Johnson wrote,

> who objected to Scrooge's conversion as too sudden and radical to be psychologically convincing. But this is to mistake a semi-serious fantasy for a piece of prosaic realism.

And as recently as 1972, Scrooge was still being discussed in the same terms. The personality transformation in *A Christmas Carol,* Joseph Gold remarks in *Charles Dickens: Radical Moralist,*

> is not much more than magical or symbolic. Indeed, by writing a fairy or ghost story, Dickens deliberately avoids dealing with the question of psychological or spiritual growth.

The Scrooge problem, as defined by these four statements, appears to be one of credibility. It is true that even the severest critic of *A Christmas Carol* is likely, thanks to Dickens' skill as a dramatist and manipulator of language, to find himself moved and almost convinced by Scrooge's change of heart. Speaking purely from the point of view of the laws of weights and measures that govern esthetics, sufficient emotional intensity is generated by the visits of the three Christmas Spirits to justify, at least within the terms of the work itself, the old man's conversion at the end, and to cause us temporarily to suspend our disbelief in the reality of that conversion. I say "almost convinced," however, because often there is a measure of discontent in even the most positive emotional response of the serious reader to this book. It is a discontent arising from the obvious disparity between the way in which moral and psychological mechanisms operate in the story and the way in which they seem to the reader to work in the "real world," a discontent focusing, as the quoted passages suggest, on the unconvincing ease and apparent permanence of Scrooge's reformation. . . .

I would like to suggest that we adopt, for the time being, the notion of Dickens as primarily a metaphysical novelist, if only because this hypothesis will permit us to account for the extraordinary power of a tale like *A Christmas Carol* in the face of the story's obvious inadequacies when judged by the more traditional standards of plausibility and "realism." For if *A Christmas Carol* is at least a partial failure as the moral fable of a man expiating years of wickedness with a few hours of generosity, or as a social document about a world in which human obligations may be satisfactorily discharged with some random charitable gestures, or as a psychological case history of a "manic-depressive" temporarily reformed by Christmas sentimentality and self-pity, then it is most certainly a success as the metaphysical study of a human being's quest for, and rediscovery of, his own innocence.

METAPHYSICAL INNOCENCE

This concept of metaphysical innocence in Dickens requires some explanation, for in his works the author also depicts many kinds of innocence that are not notably metaphysical: for example, the innocence, which is in fact a kind of stubborn and almost calculated naïveté, of Tom Pinch in *Martin Chuzzlewit*, or even of Mr. Pickwick; or the curious Victorian sexual innocence of Little Nell or Esther Summerson; or that most general and apparently self-evident of all innocence in fiction to which one critic alludes when he writes that "every central character must . . . be *relatively* innocent at the beginning of his book; that is, he must be more innocent early in the story than he is later." All these different innocences have, to make an obvious point, one thing in common: they all can be lost; indeed, they all *ought* to be lost in a well-regulated life, and once they are lost they cannot be recovered. For they all represent the absence of something important and valuable—experience, maturity—and so cannot properly be recommended to us in and of themselves without an author running the risk of sentimentality. Moreover, they all exist within a framework of the everyday "real" world of observable phenomena in which human life is commonly experienced as a linear journey from youth to age and from innocence to experience, in which the world makes a progress through time in one direction only, without possibility of return, a progress through an essentially rational universe in which nothing is more unlikely than that, to use Keats' famous phrase, "a rose should shut, and be a bud again."

Metaphysical innocence is a very different matter. It is a positive, not a negative quality; a substantial presence rather than a mere vacancy. Moreover, it is a permanent characteristic of human life and so, unlike other kinds of innocence, can never be lost. To be sure, in many lives the gradual accumulation of worldly experience may have the effect of obscuring from a man his own metaphysical innocence, of making it appear to him that that innocence has vanished along with the more ephemeral innocences of which we have been speaking. But, in fact, metaphysical innocence is immutable, retaining its original strength behind the gathering clouds of experience, and it is therefore always potentially recoverable by the individual, always ready to be *rein*troduced by him into his consciousness of himself. From this definition of innocence comes a view of life as something other than a linear movement through events, a mechanical progress from blankness to surfeit in a world in which a man is invariably "more innocent early in his story than he is later in it." Instead, this definition urges us to see life as a cyclical journey, a journey setting out from the innocence that, paradoxically, is to be the goal circling away from that innocence for the purpose of achieving, by way of contrast, a better view of it, and returning finally to the start, to where, as D.H. Lawrence puts it in his poem "Pomegranate," "the end cracks open with the beginning."

It is as difficult to define a concept like metaphysical innocence as it is to define the Christian concept of "grace," of which it is perhaps a modern analogue. In both cases, one falls inevitably into the rhetoric of mysticism. Albert Camus, however, has succeeded admirably in putting the matter in relatively practical terms. Writing, . . . in *The Myth of Sisyphus*, about what he calls "absurd" man, Camus says:

> At a certain point on his path the absurd man is tempted [to substitute faith for doubt]. History is not lacking either in religions or prophets, even without gods. He is asked to leap. All he can reply is that he doesn't fully understand, that it is not obvious. Indeed, he does not want to do anything but what he fully understands. He is assured that this is the sin of pride, but he does not understand that notion of sin; that perhaps hell is in store, but he has not enough imagination to visualize that strange future; that he is losing immortal life, but that seems to him an idle consideration. An attempt is made to get him to admit his guilt. *He feels innocent.* To tell the truth, that is all he feels—his irreparable innocence. (italics mine)

Readers will recognize in this passage a contemporary statement of the theme of the Book of Job, where also a man is urged, both by the horror of his condition and by the logic of his friends, to admit his guilt, but where, in spite of everything, he too insists upon his "irreparable innocence." The key fact about all such protestations of innocence, it should be noted, is that they are profoundly antirational. In his book *Irrational Man,* William Barrett makes the point that whenever men insist on the limits of reason, they are taking an existentialist stand. But the reverse of this statement is also true. Wherever men are found taking an existentialist stand, asserting what Camus calls their "irreparable innocence," they are insisting on the limits of reason. Interestingly, the Camus passage represents just such a quarrel between "reasonable man," who believes in a world of causality where conclusions follow necessarily and logically from premises, and "absurd man," who rejects such mechanical rationalism as a basis for human life. Job's comforters are also apostles of such a rationalism. Beginning with the premise that God is just, they conclude, logically, from the fact that Job is suffering, that he is guilty and deserves to suffer. Job, on the other hand, noting his own persistent sense of guiltlessness in the face of calamitous punishment, recognizes the radical discontinuity in the universe between a man's deeds and his fate. The moment he makes this discovery, the moment he accepts the fact that he can suffer *as if he were guilty* and still be innocent, he is freed from the burdensome rationality of his friends, from their curiously corrupting sense of justice which omits a man's own experience of himself from its moral equation, freed to be the final judge of his own worthiness and so to come again into his old legacy of wholeness and health, that original innocence from which his cyclical journey began.

The extraordinary parallels between the Book of Job and *A Christmas Carol* make it tempting to cast all the readers who have ever deplored the unreasonableness of Scrooge's conversion in the roles of Job's comforters. For the restoration of Scrooge's innocence at the end of his story, like the restoration of Job's prosperity at the end of his ordeal, seems to declare that a rose can indeed shut and be a bud again, and this is an idea no rational critic can countenance. But it is precisely this subversive, antirational point that Dickens is determined to make in his story, a story whose success is attested to by the very uneasiness with which so many readers confront their favorable responses to it.

PERFECT INNOCENCE

Though we never see Scrooge at the very beginning of his life, we may reasonably assume that, since he is a human being, he too, like all other human beings, experienced in his earliest days that infant sense, celebrated by Wordsworth in the "Immortality Ode," of his absolute continuity with the rest of the universe, his identity with everything around him. Tennyson makes this same point when he writes, in *In Memoriam*, of how

> The baby new to earth and sky
>   What time his tender palm is prest
>   Against the circle of the breast,
> Has never thought that "this is I."

Tennyson, like Wordsworth, is speaking of that phenomenological sense of wholeness in the earliest moments of life, that inability to distinguish between what is the self and what is not the self which Freud calls the "oceanic" effect and which is implicit in nearly every "myth of the beginning," not least in the Genesis story of the Garden of Eden.

In the beginning, Adam is *in* the Garden, but just as important, he is *of* the Garden, literally of its clay, and figuratively of its essence. This is the crucial point. In the profoundest sense, Adam and the Garden are coextensive. The environment that sustains the man belongs to him in exactly the way in which his body belongs to him. He need not earn his living; he need take no action to prove that he is worthy of life. He is whole—that is, healthy—in his at-oneness, and indeed, Adam's innocence in the Garden may be seen principally as a function of that wholeness. It is a function, too, of the timelessness of the Garden; for there is no death in Eden, and without death there is no direction in which time can flow. Thus Adam's innocence, like the innocence of the infant described by Wordsworth—and by extension like the innocence of Scrooge in his infancy—is an innocence of eternity and omnipresence, an innocence of perfect metaphysical health.

It is Adam's fate—man's fate—to lose that health. Specifically, Adam's "sin" is to act upon his discovery that there is a difference between his own will and the will of everything that is not himself, this latter will being called "God" in the story. His punishment is to have to live for the rest of his life with the knowledge of that difference, and his famous fall is therefore a fall out of eternity into time and out of omnipresence into the limited confines of self. The moment time appears in the world, the possibility of endings—of death—also appears. From that moment, man is committed to the process that characterizes the world of reality, the irreversible journey from birth to death. He is also burdened, through becoming aware of the difference between himself and everything else, with the curse of self-consciousness which Matthew Arnold, for one, saw as the particular plague of the post-Renaissance world ("The dialogue of the soul with itself has begun"), but which Thomas Carlyle perhaps more aptly characterized as the congenital disease of men in all ages ("Here as before, the sign of health is Unconsciousness").

ADAM'S FALL

Thrust out of Eden, the symbol of his old innocence, Adam also falls from grace. He is no longer, as he was before, *entitled* to life. Everything that was once his through the mere fact of his existence he must now struggle to regain. His universe is now a universe of causality in which, if he does not labor, he does not eat; a universe in which everything once lovingly given must now be meanly purchased. It is also, for the first time, a world of rationality and therefore of guilt, for there is no great difference between the idea that if Adam is hungry, it must be because he has not worked, and the idea that if Job is suffering, it must be because he has sinned.

When we first see Ebenezer Scrooge as a young man, he too has fallen from grace, his paradise already lost. (The story only hints at the occasion of the fall, though it does so in terms that emphasize the Edenic nature of the event. "Father is so much kinder than he used to be," says Scrooge's sister, urging the boy to return to the family, "that home's like heaven.") Under the aegis of the Spirit of Christmas Past, the old miser sees himself as a young boy seated alone in an empty schoolroom, rejected by his companions, reading stories about Ali Baba, and Robinson Crusoe, and the Sultan's Groom turned upside down by the Genii. The images all confirm the postlapsarian nature of the scene. The boy is alone, driven from his own world, shades of the prison house of self already falling about him. He sits in an empty schoolroom, empty not just because the others have left, but empty metaphorically as well, for it is not through any logic of the school that Scrooge's old health will be regained. Rather, that logic is itself the disease, though he does not yet know it.

In his loneliness, the young Scrooge tries to recapture, through the exercise of his imagination, which is a form of memory, the lost state of grace, his books the vehicles of that magical return. Ali Baba, the fabulous Arab who comes into his rich legacy through the mere pronouncement of a magic word, is a particularly poignant symbol of Scrooge's own desire. Robinson Crusoe, on the other hand, forecasts more realistically the young man's future, representing as he does the triumph of bourgeois enterprise, the achievement of material success after a lifetime of lonely labor on a desert island. And it is Scrooge himself, the old man, faithful Groom of his great Sultan, Money, who in the end will be turned upside down by the Genii of the Spirit of Christmas.

A LIFE OF ACQUISITION

Soon enough, Scrooge decides that books are no answer to his problem; indeed, they only exacerbate it. When one has lost something precious, it seems clear to the young man, one must labor to get it back. Magic and nostalgia will not restore it, only hard work will even begin to recover the lost legacy, as Adam was the first to find out. Scrooge, too, learns this lesson and plunges early into a life of acquisition, as if by accumulating one by one all the elements of his lost paradise, he could reconstruct it whole one day and live in it again. This is the rationale of his miserliness, a miserliness that we must therefore see not as a sign of his depravity but rather as an indication of how passionate is his desire to recover his lost innocence.

His commitment to a life of accumulation, to the typical Victorian metaphysic of rational materialism, becomes final in the scene in which a somewhat older Scrooge, still in the prime of life but with signs of "care and avarice" already in his face, breaks painfully with his fiancée. Actually, it is she who breaks with him, bringing out into the open a truth which for years both have recognized in silence: that any passion the young man may once have had for her has long since been supplanted by the passion for gain. Given Scrooge's fate, this is necessarily so. For having won the girl, he cannot be satisfied with her, since she represents only a part of what he lost when he lost his "oceanic" innocence, and he cannot rest until he has recovered it all. In "Ulysses," Tennyson seemingly makes a virtue of this insatiable longing for wholeness, but where Tennyson was writing, at least in part, about the triumph of post-Renaissance, Faustian man, Dickens was writing about his tragedy.

The girl tells Scrooge that he has changed ("When [our contract] was made," she says, "you were another man"). Her statement defines Scrooge's fallen condition. There is no change in Eden, but in the world men change day by day, all their days linked to one another logically and causally until they forge the heavy chain that weighs down the ghost of Jacob Marley—who continues to exist in time even after his death—and that in the end sinks everyone implicated in its logic. Scrooge acquiesces wholeheartedly in his enchainment, imagining, curiously, that with the addition of each new link he is moving closer to his old freedom and health. This belief is the clue to all his behavior: his miserliness, his insistence upon punctuality, his terror of losing even one day of work at Christmas, his treatment of the men who come to ask for charity. This latter scene is very important in any analysis of the story. Everyone recalls Scrooge's famous reply to the request for alms for the poor: "Are there no prisons? Are there no workhouses?" For Scrooge, prisons and workhouses, the machinery that a rational society has constructed to deal with the problem of the poor, are consonant with his own rational commitment to life. Charity, on the other hand, is entirely subversive of that commitment, destroying the crucial connection between cause and effect, suggesting that a man has a right to live even if he has not earned that right and can offer no logical proof that he deserves it. To do him justice, Scrooge applies the same hard standards to himself. When it is he who is being offered the charity of his nephew's affection, he rejects such unearned love as peremptorily as he refuses to give it to others. For, monomaniacally, Scrooge keeps his eye always on his one great goal, to get back to his first home, a goal he long ago decided could be reached only as other, more worldly goals are reached—by logically calculating the shortest road to it and then by walking down that road one logical step at a time.

SCROOGE'S MISTAKE

That this strategy is radically mistaken is the whole point of the story; that such a rational road as Scrooge travels leads only away from his old home and toward death is Dickens' Christmas lesson. It is a lesson that has been taught many times before—in the story of the Tower of Babel, for example. The men who attempted to build a tower to God were not guilty of that "sin of pride" of which Camus is so contemptuous. Their impulse was understandable and even legitimate, very much like Scrooge's. They sought only to get back home and recover lost innocence, which they quite properly associated with God. But their strategy was wrong. They supposed that they could get to heaven by putting one brick on top of another, that they could reach infinity through finite means, that they could communicate with eternity in the language of time. Thus, the confusion of tongues, which the Bible says *followed* the attempt to build the tower, in fact preceded it.

Scrooge's problem too is one of a confusion of tongues. He too tries to reach infinity through finite means, to recover wholeness by collecting parts, to arrive at eternity by moving through time. He believes that the world of material reality is the only reality there is, and therefore, along with so many of his fellow post-Renaissance men, supposes that if anything important is to be accomplished, it must be accomplished in terms of that material reality—by manipulating it, cataloging it, buying and selling it—and by applying the rational laws which the study of that material reality discovers. And, significantly, no one is more thoroughly taken in by this idea than the reader of *A Christmas Carol.* For Dickens' great triumph as an artist in this tale is to get us to *see* Scrooge's mistake in the story by causing us first to *make* that mistake ourselves.

We mistakenly suppose, for example, that Scrooge is an old man. It is a natural enough mistake, one to which Hamlet, for example, calls attention when he tells Polonius of how

> the satirical rogue says here that old men have grey beards, that their faces are wrinkled, their eyes purging thick amber and plum-tree gum.

When we see a man with such infirmities, slow of movement and set in his ways, we naturally call him old. He has lived many years since his birth, and the chance of his

SCROOGE'S SECULAR CONVERSION

Don Richard Cox writes that A Christmas Carol *is a story with a "rather secular twist," arguing that Scrooge does not achieve a state of metaphysical innocence but rather exchanges one set of economic values for another.*

The "conversion" that Scrooge experiences is not a holy revelation but an economic revelation. Scrooge saves his soul in the same way that Pickwick so often finds atonement—he spends money. Scrooge buys a turkey for the Cratchits—the biggest and most expensive one there is—tips the boy excessively, and then chuckles with happiness as he pays for a cab to send both boy and turkey to the Cratchits. He then promises a generous sum to the poor (whispering the exact figure gleefully in the ear of the gentleman he had previously kicked out of his office). Scrooge then raises Cratchit's salary and promises future aid to Cratchit's family. To further ensure salvation Scrooge performs one last act of contrition: he buys some more coal. The final illustration of the book shows Scrooge sharing a steaming bowl of punch before a roaring fire, and we need no further proof that Scrooge has mended his ways; he has now learned to spend money and enjoy the material comforts of life. After all, even the Cratchit family knows the true meaning of Christmas; only Bob and Tiny Tim attend church while the rest of the Cratchits stay at home and prepare the food that will presumably fulfill both the physical and spiritual needs of them all.

Elliot L. Gilbert quite accurately points out that Scrooge has made himself a "commitment to a life of accumulation, to the typical Victorian metaphysic of rational materialism." In this respect, Scrooge is not too much unlike his young creator, who with his resplendent waistcoats and somewhat gaudy dress demonstrated in his own lifestyle that materialistic rewards were indeed the legacy to be found by those who adopted a doctrine of hard work. Scrooge does not return to a state of innocence, I would suggest, nor does he really undergo a spiritual or moral conversion. Scrooge simply exchanges one set of economic values for another; in doing so, he comes to the rather secular conclusion that it is not money that brings happiness in life, but rather what money can buy. He has not truly become "innocent," but then he never was really very "wicked" either.

Don Richard Cox, *PMLA*, October 1975.

returning to the innocence of those old days seems remote indeed. Even more remote, we would suppose, is the chance of his changing his long-established ways. After the merriment of his nephew's house—even during it—Scrooge will surely sink back into "moroseness, vindictiveness, suspicion." This is what can realistically be expected of such an old man.

But to analyze the story in these terms is to accept the very principles of rational materialism which it is the purpose of the story to undermine. For Scrooge is not in fact an old man; it is only a satirical rogue who would say so. With the exception of the events in the brief prologue and epilogue, the whole of his life is actually lived in the course of one night; if he is of any age at all, he is barely half-a-dozen hours old. Chronology, in short, is an illusion, the story tells us, one of the illusions man suffers from when he falls out of eternity into time. But time, which is therefore the enemy, can be defeated by a phenomenological insight into the simultaneity of all experience; defeated as Scrooge himself defeats it when, immediately upon awakening from his dream, he cries out, "I will live in the Past, the Present, and the Future! The spirits of all Three shall strive within me." In truth, of course, he has always lived simultaneously in the past, the present, and the future, as all men do. It is only the immediacy, the insistence of material reality, Dickens tells us, that distracts men from the greater reality of their inner lives. Marley's chains, could he have but known it, were only "mind-forged manacles" after all.

That the past, present, and future exist in an eternal present is made clear in a number of other ways in the story. Christmas Past, Christmas Present, and Christmas Yet to Come, for example, exist simultaneously between the stroke of midnight and the stroke of one. Again, one of Dickens' favorite devices, appearing memorably, for example, in *Dombey and Son,* is the use of a child and an adult together in a story to represent the same character at different stages of his life, but with the two existing—as if to underscore the metaphysical point of the story—simultaneously. Tiny Tim and Scrooge have that kind of a relationship in *A Christmas Carol,* the rejected child of Scrooge's memory of himself being actualized in the crippled boy with whom, through Bob Cratchit, the old miser has an inescapable rapport. It is, for example, in the vision of the future in which Scrooge sees

his own grave that Tiny Tim is also dead. In the alternate future, on the other hand, in which Scrooge reforms, Tiny Tim
is cured and flourishes. The boy whom Scrooge sends for
the turkey on Christmas morning participates in this same
symbolism. The boy's nimbleness presages the coming nimbleness of Tiny Tim, and Scrooge's complimentary references to him as "a remarkable boy, a delightful boy," apply
at least as much to himself, in his new-found youthfulness,
as to the young turkey-bearer. "I'm quite a baby," Scrooge
cries. "Never mind. I don't care. I'd rather be a baby."

ETERNAL CHILDHOOD

This is not mere giddiness on Scrooge's part, likely to vanish
when the manic phase gives way to the depressive. It is,
rather, a very precise statement of the man's most persistent
ambition. His whole life has been a quest for the lost innocence, the lost wholeness of his infancy. He has always, in
one sense, wanted to be a baby, but time has kept defeating
him, bearing him further and further from his goal as long
as he believed in its power. The moment, however, that
Scrooge decides to live simultaneously in the past, present
and future, time loses all its terrors for him and all its power
over him. He is no longer borne ruthlessly away by it in one
direction only. As the master of time now, he can move
freely through it in any direction. He can *be* a baby because
he *is* a baby, as much as he is a man of any other age. The
experience, we know, is a common one; no one, whatever
his years, ever quite loses a sense of himself as the child he
once was. One recalls Rostov in *War and Peace* lying
wounded on the battlefield, hearing the French soldiers ap-
proaching to finish him off, and finding it genuinely astonishing that they should be coming to kill him, the good child,
whom his father and mother love.

It is from this universal sense of eternal childhood and "irreparable innocence" that Scrooge's change of heart derives
its conviction. We must not let ourselves be embarrassed into
questioning the durability of that change, on a metaphysical
level, by psychoanalytic critics who are still trapped in a rationalism that both Scrooge and Dickens have been at such
pains to overcome. The burden of the psychoanalytic argument is that Scrooge has been a hardened old man so long
that no real change in him is possible. But if we agree with
Wordsworth, as well as with Dickens, that "the Child is father

of the Man," then in fact Scrooge has been a child much longer than he has been a person of any other age, and we can trust him not to ignore again his most venerable self.

That venerable child now shows Scrooge the way home he has been seeking. During the visit of the Spirit of Christmas Past, the old man is brought to recall a day when his life at school was interrupted by the sudden arrival of his sister.

> A little girl, much younger than the boy, came darting in, and putting her arms about his neck, and often kissing him, addressed him as her "Dear, dear brother."
>
> "I have come to bring you home, dear brother!" said the child, clapping her tiny hands, and bending down to laugh. "To bring you home, home, home!"
>
> "Home, little Fan?" returned the boy.
>
> "Yes," said the child, brimful of glee. "Home, for good and all. Home, forever and ever."

Years later the sister's son, Scrooge's nephew Fred, renews his mother's old offer of rescue. "Don't be angry, Uncle," the young man says, having dropped in on Scrooge at the office to wish him a Merry Christmas, and having received only grim lectures and repeated shouts of "Humbug!" in return. "Come, dine with us tomorrow."

As we have seen, it is impossible at this point for Scrooge to accept such a charitable invitation from his nephew. For to the old man, such unsolicited generosity, requiring nothing in return, is an anomaly in a material universe where everything must be bought and paid for, and is thus a threat to the very order of his existence. That such an act of grace epitomizes the innocence whose loss Scrooge feels so keenly and toward the recovery of which his whole life of frenzied acquisitiveness has been directed is a fact he still has to learn; and had he been called upon, at this point, to define the home for which he was secretly yearning, he probably could have done no better than to reply, with Robert Frost's dour farmer in "The Death of the Hired Man," that

> Home is the place where, when you have to go there,
> They have to take you in.

Only later, after the visits of the three Christmas Spirits, and after his literal rejuvenation, could Scrooge have understood the compassionate rejoinder of the farmer's wife:

>   I should have called it
> Something you somehow haven't to deserve.

That very night, Scrooge appears hesitantly at the door of his nephew's house, still enough of a rationalist to wonder what he can expect at the hands of one from whom he deserves so little. Fred's gracious welcome dispels all doubt. The answer had been there for the taking all along, even as early as the sister's invitation to come "Home for good and all. Home, forever and ever," but it had been necessary for Scrooge to make his cyclical journey. Now, with time once more his servant rather than his master, and with everything of value already his without his asking, he returns to the state of metaphysical innocence from which he started, and his history comes to an end.

A Christmas Carol and the Economic Man

Edgar Johnson

> Edgar Johnson emphasizes the social implications of
> *A Christmas Carol,* calling the story "a serio-comic
> parable of social redemption." According to Johnson,
> Dickens uses Scrooge as an emblem to indict a cal-
> lous economic philosophy that is heartlessly indiffer-
> ent to the welfare of human beings. Scrooge's con-
> version, then, is more than one individual's change
> of heart: It is Dickens's plea for mankind to broaden
> the sense of brotherhood and fellowship characteris-
> tic of the Christmas season. Edgar Johnson is the au-
> thor of *Charles Dickens: His Tragedy and Triumph.*

Everyone knows Dickens' *Christmas Carol* for its colorful
painting of a rosy fireside good cheer and warmth of feeling,
made all the more vivid by the contrasting chill wintry darkness in which its radiant scenes are framed. Most readers
realize too how characteristic of all Dickens' sentiments
about the Christmas season are the laughter and tenderness
and jollity he poured into the *Carol.* What is not so widely
understood is that it was also consistently and deliberately
created as a critical blast against the very rationale of industrialism and its assumptions about the organizing principles
of society. It is an attack upon both the economic behavior of
the nineteenth century business man and the supporting
theory of doctrinaire utilitarianism. As such it is a good deal
more significant than the mere outburst of warmhearted
sentimentality it is often taken to be.

THE SPIRIT OF CHRISTMAS

Its sharper intent is, indeed, ingeniously disguised. Not even
the festivities at Dingley Dell, in *Pickwick Papers,* seem to

Excerpted from "The *Christmas Carol* and the Economic Man," by Edgar Johnson, *The
American Scholar,* Winter 1951–52, vol. 21. Copyright © 1952 by the Phi Beta Kappa
Society. Reprinted with permission from *The American Scholar.*

have a more genial innocence than the scenes of the *Christmas Carol.* It is full of the tang of snow and cold air and crisp green holly-leaves, and warm with the glow of crimson holly-berries, blazing hearths, and human hearts. Deeper than this, however, Dickens makes of the Christmas spirit a symbolic criticism of the relations that throughout almost all the rest of the year subsist among men. It is a touchstone, revealing and drawing forth the gold of generosity ordinarily crusted over with selfish habit, an earnest of the truth that our natures are not entirely or even essentially devoted to competitive struggle.

Dickens is certain that the enjoyment most men are able to feel in the happiness of others can play a larger part than it does in the tenor of their lives. The sense of brotherhood, he feels, can be broadened to a deeper and more active concern for the welfare of all mankind. It is in this light that Dickens sees the Spirit of Christmas. So understood, as the distinguished scholar Professor Louis Cazamian rightly points out, his "philosophie de Noël" becomes the very core of his social thinking.

Not that Christmas has for Dickens more than the very smallest connection with Christian dogma or theology. It involves no conception of the virgin birth or transubstantiation or sacrificial atonement or redemption by faith. For Dickens Christmas is primarily a human, not a supernatural, feast, with glowing emphasis on goose and gravy, plum-pudding and punch, mistletoe and kissing-games, dancing and frolic, as well as open-handedness, sympathy, and warmth of heart. Dickens does not believe that love of others demands utter abnegation or mortification of the flesh; it is not sadness but joyful fellowship. The triumphal meaning of Christmas peals in the angel voices ringing through the sky: "On earth peace, good will to men." It is a sign that men do not live by bread alone, that they do not live for barter and sale alone. No way of life is either true or rewarding that leaves out men's need of loving and of being loved.

THE PURSUIT OF PROFIT

The theme of the *Christmas Carol* is thus closely linked with the theme of *Martin Chuzzlewit,* which was being written and published as a serial during the very time in which the shorter story appeared. The selfishness so variously manifested in the one is limited in the other to the selfishness of financial gain. For in an acquisitive society the form that selfishness predominantly takes is monetary greed. The purpose of such a society is the protection of property rights. Its rules are created by those who have money and power, and are designed, to the extent that they are consistent, for the perpetuation of money and power. With the growing importance of commerce in the eighteenth century, and of industry in the nineteenth, political economists—the "philosophers" Dickens detested—rationalized the spirit of ruthless greed into a system claiming authority throughout society.

Services as well as goods, they said, were subject only to the laws of profitable trade. There was no just price. One bought in the cheapest market and sold in the dearest. There was no just wage. The mill owner paid the mill hand what competition decreed under the determination of the "iron law of wage." If the poor, the insufficiently aggressive, and the mediocre in ability were unable to live on what they could get, they must starve—or put up with the treadmill and the workhouse—and even these institutions represented concessions to mere humanity that must be made as forbidding as possible. Ideally, no sentimental conceptions must be allowed to obstruct the workings of the law of supply and demand. "Cash-nexus" was the sole bond between man and man. The supreme embodiment of this social theory was the notion of the "economic man," that curiously fragmentary picture of human nature, who never performed any action except at the dictates of monetary gain. And Scrooge, in the *Christmas Carol*, is nothing other than a personification of economic man.

SCROOGE AS ECONOMIC MAN

Scrooge's entire life is limited to cash-boxes, ledgers and bills of sale. He underpays and bullies and terrifies his clerk, and grudges him even enough coal in his office fire to keep warm. All sentiment, kindness, generosity, tenderness, he dismisses as humbug. All imagination he regards as a species of mental indigestion. He feels that he has discharged his full duty to society in contributing his share of the taxes that pay for the prison, the workhouse, the operation of the treadmill and the poor law, and he bitterly resents having his pocket picked to keep even them going. The out-of-work and the indigent sick are to him merely idle and useless; they had better die and decrease the surplus population. So entirely does Scrooge exemplify the economic man that, like that abstraction, his grasping rapacity has ceased to have any purpose beyond itself: when he closes up his office for the night he takes his pinched heart off to a solitary dinner at a tavern and then to his bleak chambers where he sits alone over his gruel.

Now from one angle, of course, *A Christmas Carol* indicts the economic philosophy represented by Scrooge for its unhappy influence on society. England's prosperity was not so uncertain—if, indeed, any nation's ever is—that she needed to be parsimonious and cruel to her waifs and strays, or even to the incompetents and casualties of life. To neglect the poor, to deny them education, to give them no protection from covetous employers, to let them be thrown out of work and fall ill and die in filthy surroundings that then engender spreading pestilence, to allow them to be harried by misery into crime—all these turn out in the long run to be the most disastrous shortsightedness.

That is what the Ghost of Christmas Present means in showing Scrooge the two ragged and wolfish children glaring from beneath its robes. "They are Man's," says the Spirit. "And they cling to me, appealing from their fathers. This boy is Ignorance. This girl is Want. Beware them both, and all of their degree, but most of all beware this boy, for on his brow I see that written which is Doom, unless the writing be erased." And when Scrooge asks if they have no refuge, the Spirit ironically echoes his own words: "Are there no prisons? Are there no workhouses?"

DICKENS' VISION

Scrooge's relation with his clerk Bob Cratchit is another illustration of the same point. To say, as some commentators have done, that Scrooge is paying Cratchit all he is worth on the open market (or he would get another job) is to assume the very conditions Dickens is attacking. It is not only that timid, uncompetitive people like Bob Cratchit may lack the courage to bargain for their rights. But, as Dickens knows well, there are many things other than the usefulness of a man's work that determine his wage—the existence, for example, of a large body of other men able to do the same job. And if Cratchit is getting the established remuneration for his work, that makes the situation worse, not better; for instead of an isolated one, his is a general case. What Dickens has at heart is not any economic conception like Marx's labor theory of value, but a feeling of the human value of human beings. Unless a man is a noxious danger to society, Dickens feels, a beast of prey to be segregated or destroyed; if he is able and willing to work, whatever the work may be—he is entitled at least to enough for him to live on, by the mere virtue of his humanity alone.

But the actual organization that Dickens saw in society callously disregarded all such humane principles. The hardened criminal was maintained in jail with more care than the helpless debtor who had broken no law. The pauper who owed nobody, but whom age, illness or industrial change might have thrown out of work, was treated more severely than many a debtor and jailbird. And the poor clerk or laborer, rendered powerless by his need or the number of others like him, could be held to a pittance barely sufficient to keep him and his family from starvation.

Against such inequities Dickens maintains that any work worth doing should be paid enough to maintain a man and his family without grinding worry. How are the Bob Cratchits and their helpless children to live? Or are we to let the crippled Tiny Tims die and decrease the surplus population? "Man," says the Ghost, "if man you be in heart, not adamant, forbear that wicked cant until you have discovered What the surplus is and Where it is. . . . It may be, that in the sight of Heaven, you are more worthless and less fit to live than millions like this poor man's child. Oh God! to hear the Insect on the leaf pronouncing on the too much life among his hungry brothers in the dust!"

Coldhearted arrogance and injustice storing up a dangerous heritage of poverty and ignorance—such is Dickens' judgment of the economic system that Scrooge exemplifies. But its consequences do not end with the cruelties it inflicts upon the masses of the people or the evils it works in society. It injures Scrooge as well. All the more generous impulses of humanity he has stifled and mutilated in himself. All natural affection he has crushed. The lonely boy he used to be, weeping in school, the tender brother, the eager youth, the young man who once fell disinterestedly in love with a dowerless girl—what has he done to them in making himself into a money-making machine, as hard and sharp as flint, and frozen with the internal ice that clutches his shriveled heart? That dismal cell, his office, and his gloomy rooms, are only a prison within which he dwells self-confined, barred and close-locked as he drags a chain of his own cash-boxes and dusty ledgers. Acting on a distortedly inadequate conception of self-interest, Scrooge has deformed and crippled himself to bitter sterility.

And Scrooge's fallacy is the fallacy of organized society. Like his house, which Dickens fancifully imagines playing hide-and-seek with other houses when it was a young house, and losing its way in a blind alley it has forgotten how to get out of, Scrooge has lost his way between youth and maturity. Society too in the course of its development has gone astray and then hardened itself in obdurate error with a heartless economic theory. Scrooge's conversion is more than the transformation of a single human being. It is a plea for society itself to undergo a change of heart.

Dickens does not, it should be noticed, take the uncompromising position that the self-regarding emotions are to be eradicated altogether. He is not one of those austere theorists who hold that the individual must be subordinated to the state or immolate himself to the service of an abstract humanity. Concern for one's self and one's own welfare is necessary and right, but true self-love cannot be severed from love of others without growing barren and diseased. Only in the communion of brotherhood is it healthy and fruitful. When Scrooge has truly changed, and has dispatched the anonymous gift of the turkey to Bob Cratchit as an earnest of repentance, his next move is to go to his nephew's house and ask wistfully, "Will you let me in, Fred?" With love reanimated in his heart, he may hope for love.

There have been readers who objected to Scrooge's conversion as too sudden and radical to be psychologically convincing. But this is to mistake a semi-serious fantasy for a piece of prosaic realism. Even so, the emotions in Scrooge to which the Ghosts appeal are no unsound means to the intended end: the awakened memories of a past when he had known gentler and warmer ties than in any of his later years, the realization of his exclusion from all kindness and affection in others now, the fears of a future when he may be lonelier and more unloved still. And William James in *The Varieties of Religious Experience* provides scores of case-histories that parallel both the suddenness of Scrooge's conversion and the sense of radiant joy he feels in the world around him after it has taken place. It may be that what really gives the skeptics pause is that Scrooge is converted to a gospel of good cheer. They could probably believe easily enough if he espoused some gloomy doctrine of intolerance.

ALLEGORY

But it is doubtful whether such questions ever arise when one is actually reading the *Christmas Carol*. From the very beginning Dickens strikes a tone of playful exaggeration that warns us this is no exercise in naturalism. Scrooge carries "his own low temperature always about with him; he iced his office in the dog-days." Blind men's dogs, when they see him coming, tug their masters into doorways to avoid him. The entire world of the story is an animistic one: houses play hide-and-seek, door-knockers come to life as human heads, the tuning of a fiddle is "like fifty stomach aches," old Fezziwig's legs wink as he dances, potatoes bubbling in a saucepan knock loudly at the lid "to be let out and peeled." Scrooge's own language has a jocose hyperbole, even when he is supposed to be most ferocious or most terrified, that makes his very utterance seem half a masquerade. "If I could work my will," he snarls, "every idiot who goes about with 'Merry Christmas' on his lips should be boiled with his own pudding, and buried with a stake of holly through his heart. He should!" Is that the accent of a genuine curmudgeon or of a man trying to sound more violent than he feels? And to Marley's Ghost, despite his disquiet, he remarks, "You may be an undigested bit of beef, a blob of mustard, a crumb of cheese, a fragment of an underdone potato. There's more of gravy than of grave about you, whatever you are!"

   All these things make it clear that Dickens—as always when he is most deeply moved and most profound—is speaking in terms of unavowed allegory. But the allegory of Dickens is in one way subtler than the allegory of writers like Kafka or Melville. Kafka is always hinting the existence of hidden meanings by making the experience of his characters so baffling and irrational on a merely realistic level that we are obliged to search for symbolic significances. And Melville, too, by a score of devices, from those rolling, darkly magnificent and extraordinary soliloquies to the mystery of Ahab's intense and impassioned pursuit of the White Whale, forces us to realize that this is a more metaphysical duel than one with a mere deep-sea beast.

Dickens, however, leaves his surface action so entirely clear and the behavior of his characters so plain that they do not puzzle us into groping for gnomic meanings. Scrooge is a miser, his nephew a warmhearted fellow, Bob Cratchit a poor clerk—what could be simpler? If there is a touch of oddity in the details, that is merely Dickens' well-known comic grotesquerie; if Scrooge's change of heart is sharp and antithetical, that is only Dickens' melodramatic sentimentality. Surely all the world knows that Dickens is never profound?

SOCIAL REDEMPTION

But the truth is that Dickens has so fused his abstract thought and its imaginative forming that one melts almost entirely into the other. Though our emotional perception of Dickens' meaning is immediate and spontaneous, nothing in his handling thrusts upon us an intellectual statement of that meaning. But more than a warm-hearted outpouring of holiday sentiment, the *Christmas Carol* is in essence a serio-comic parable of social redemption. Marley's Ghost is the symbol of divine grace, and the three Christmas Spirits are the working of that grace through the agencies of memory, example and fear. And Scrooge, although of course he is himself too, is not himself alone: he is the embodiment of all that concentration upon material power and callous indifference to the welfare of human beings that the economists had erected into a system, businessmen and industrialists pursued relentlessly, and society taken for granted as inevitable and proper. The conversion of Scrooge is an image of the conversion for which Dickens hopes among mankind.

Scrooge's Dreams

William E. Morris

William E. Morris argues that critics are misguided
when they question the validity of Scrooge's conversion. To Morris, Scrooge's visions are merely
dreams, and thus originate in the recesses of
Scrooge's mind. As a product of Scrooge's own subconscious, then, the visions that prompt Scrooge's
conversion are entirely authentic and believably motivated. For example, Scrooge's fear that he will be
forgotten manifests itself in his dream visions. In this
mode, Morris analyzes the recurring motifs—fog,
darkness, and cold, for instance—that run through
Scrooge's dreams. Morris was associate professor of
English at the University of South Florida when he
contributed the following critical essay to *Studies in
Short Fiction.*

As everyone knows, being called a "scrooge" is bad. When la-
beled like this, one is considered "a tight-fisted hand at the
grindstone. . . . Hard and sharp as flint, from which no steel
had ever struck out generous fire; secret, and self-contained,
and solitary as an oyster." In reality, and in short, one is a
party-pooper, afflicted with general overtones of inhumanity.

This is the popular definition of the word *Scrooge,* and it is
unfairly the usual description of Charles Dickens' Ebenezer
Scrooge, of "A Christmas Carol." Scrooge's conversion to a
permanent goodness, which is every bit up to those impossible standards met by the totally admirable Cheerybles and
Mr. Brownlow, seems to have been utterly forgotten, or ig-
nored. Popularly lost is Dickens' last word on Scrooge: ". . .
it was always said of him that he knew how to keep a Christmas well, if any man alive possessed the knowledge." By
common consent Scrooge has been a villain at every Christmas season since 1843. Indeed, that reformed old gentleman
might well answer, " 'It's not convenient, and it's not fair.' "

What "we" remember about "A Christmas Carol" is the flinty employer, the humbly simple (and sentimental) clerk, and sweet Tiny Tim. If the general reading public remembers Scrooge's conversion at all, it sees the alteration as a punishment brought about and maintained through fear. The conversion is seen as only a part of the story, when in fact it is what the story is *all* about. "A Christmas Carol" is not, as some readers seem to think, "The Little Lame Prince" or "The Confidential Clerk." It is the reawakening of a Christian soul, although (as Edgar Johnson makes clear) it is not a religious conversion. Religious or not, the story is a celebration of an important conversion, the sort of conversion on which Dickens pinned his hopes for social, moral, economic, and even political recovery in England. The carol sung here is a song of celebration for a Christmas birth that offers hope; it is not a song of thanks for revenge accomplished or for luck had by the poor. To be an "old Scrooge" is, in the final analysis, a good thing to be. And with careful rereading of the tale the clichés of a hasty public would surely disappear.

What is more damagingly unfair than the popular mistake is the critics' treatment of Scrooge's conversion, which ranges from Edgar Johnson's insistence that Scrooge is "nothing other than a personification of economic man" to Humphry House's assertion that "his conversion, moreover, seems to be complete at a stroke, his actions after it uniform." At the critics' hands the enlightenment of Scrooge is not individual, believable, real, or even interesting. Perhaps the most surprising comment is this one by Chesterton:

> Scrooge is not really inhuman at the beginning any more than he is at the end. There is a heartiness in his inhospitable sentiments that is akin to humour and therefore inhumanity; he is only a crusty old bachelor, and had (I strongly suspect) given away turkeys secretly all his life. The beauty and the real blessing of the story do not lie in the mechanical plot of it, the repentance of Scrooge, probable or improbable; they lie in the great furnace of real unhappiness that glows through Scrooge and everything round him; that great furnace, the heart of Dickens. Whether the Christmas visions would or would not convert Scrooge, they convert us.

It is my contention that the story records the psychological—if overnight—change in Scrooge from a mechanical tool that has been manufactured by the economic institutions around him to the human being he was before business dehumanized him. His conversion is his alone, not that of "economic man"; Dickens does not intend Scrooge's awakening to be a promise for all covetous old sinners, but only a possibility to be individually hoped for. Further, if the visitations by Marley and the three spirits be accepted as dreams ("Marley was dead, to begin with. There is no doubt whatever about that."), their substance, as well as their messages and their effects, must have come from the recesses of Scrooge's own mind. And finally, if the conversion comes from within Scrooge, it could have been effected at a stroke, for surely it had been subconsciously fermenting for a long time. Of such things Christmas miracles, or epiphanies, may very well be made. Scrooge explains it: " 'I haven't missed it. The spirits have done it all in one night. They can do anything they like. Of course they can!' "

SCROOGE'S DREAM

From the Marley-faced doorknocker to the third Phantom's hood and dress shrinking, collapsing, and dwindling down to the bed post, Scrooge is dreaming, awake and asleep. The entire substance of the dreams has been all of Scrooge's own making; he has, in an agitated state, conjured up those things that he has until now hidden from himself but has not been unaware of: his own compounded sins, and Marley's; his happy and sad boyhood; his small sister and the memory of an unkind father; the gay times working under old Fezziwig on a Christmas long ago; Scrooge's denial of Belle, the girl he was to have married; the supposed or heard-of later happiness of the same girl (at Christmas, of course), married to another man; the eve of Marley's death; the Christmas gaiety of common people at the present Christmas season (which he had known, for he spoke harshly of it at his place of business only that afternoon); the happy Cratchit home this Christmas, with its touching sight of Tiny Tim and the blight of the subdued Cratchit opinion of Scrooge; Christmas present with miners, lighthouse keepers, and seamen—all more content than Scrooge despite their condition; the bright games at the Christmas home of his nephew, a place to which he was invited and angrily refused a few hours ago; the sight of the two tattered children under the Spirit's robes—the boy Ignorance, the girl Want; his own cheap funeral and the theft of his possessions; the scorn of him among business men; the death of Tiny Tim and the view of

Scrooge's own tombstone. All these would have been known to him, through experience, imagination, or the public press or gossip.

The dream visions are connected, as dreams, not only to what he knew or feared or imagined, but to each other through recurring scenes, motifs, verbal expressions, and physical props. They are believably motivated—that is, if dreams are ever believably motivated.

PERVASIVE COLD

In Stave One, before Scrooge goes to sleep, Dickens presents several clues to what trouble his dreams; we can infer the other clues from the dreams themselves. First the reader learns that this afternoon is cold, foggy, and dark. And during the dreams cold, fog, and darkness persist and dominate until they are the atmosphere of the dreams. Cold, which dominates the day, runs through the dreams, relieved only by and for persons who share each other's company. It is not relieved for Scrooge, who in his dreams can no longer use the imagination which Dickens says he relied upon to defeat cold at his counting-house. Cold is the most persistent element in the story—more pervasive than even the fog and darkness. It is the temperature of the world that cannot be shed or blown away by anyone but must be lived with and among. It is triumphed over only by the philanthropy of fellowship (which might be more specifically called kindness, love, tolerance, and sympathy between individual persons), not by the misanthropy of solitaries or the collective bargaining of institutions (" 'I help to support the establishments I have mentioned—they cost enough: and those who are badly off must go there,' " explains Scrooge). Here is that assertion dramatized:

> The cold became intense. In the main street, at the corner of the court, some labourers were repairing the gas-pipes, and had lighted a great fire in a brazier, round which a party of ragged men and boys were gathered: warming their hands and winking their eyes before the blaze in rapture. The water-plug being left in solitude, its overflowing suddenly congealed, and turned to misanthropic ice.

The great fire in the brazier of the workmen is the exact opposite of Scrooge's "very small fire" and the one he allows his clerk ("it looked like one coal"); their rapture is not at all like Scrooge's grouchiness and gloom. In contrast to the laborers', Scrooge's overflowings are congealed and turned to misanthropic ice, like the water-plug left in solitude. It is the solitude of Scrooge that has congealed him so that no out-side force of weather knows where to have him. It could not be less open to the warmth that in this story is equated to hu-man companionship.

And yet Scrooge does feel the cold, in spite of what people thought. He has caught cold in the head; he does bundle up; he does sit close to the small fire in his chambers and brood over it. The denial of cold as an economic hindrance is part of a public role that he has taken on as he has slipped into isolation. Fuel costs money just as warmth costs human feeling; and human feeling leads into a world which he has come to foreswear. "What shall I put you down for?" asks one of the gentlemen who come in the spirit of charity to col-lect money for the needy on Christmas Eve. " 'Nothing!' Scrooge replied. 'You wish to be anonymous?' 'I wish to be left alone,' said Scrooge." What Scrooge comes to see (and thus the reason for his conversion) is that if one is left alone he does become anonymous. Over and over in the dreams, this is Scrooge's fear: that he will be left and forgotten, that he will die and no one will care. This fear grows as the sug-gestion of anonymity recurs more frequently during the course of the dreams. Defense against cold is the first de-mand Scrooge makes of Bob Cratchit on the day after Christ-mas, for a fully awakened Scrooge says, " 'Make up the fires and buy another coal-scuttle before you dot another i, Bob Cratchit!' " At last Scrooge has determined to keep human warmth about him.

Fog and Darkness Motifs

Fog and darkness become symbols for incommunication and isolation in the dreams; their opposites become symbols for communication and integration with mankind. Light and clarity of vision are subdued, except in flashes of Christmas past when Scrooge is a schoolboy at play, or a young man at old Fezziwig's party, or an onlooker at Belle's happy home. These flashes are only glimmers in a usually dark atmos-phere. One of the few bright outdoor scenes is the one in which Scrooge is shown himself playing as a boy: "The city had entirely disappeared. Not a vestige of it was to be seen. The darkness and the mist had vanished with it, for it was a clear, cold, winter day, with snow upon the ground." But, as the Spirit of Christmas Past reminds him, "These are but shadows of the things that have been." Fog and darkness dominate until the last section of the story, when Scrooge awakes on Christmas morning and puts his head out the window to find, "No fog, no mist; clear, bright, jovial, stirring cold; cold piping for the blood to dance to; golden sunlight; heavenly day; sweet fresh air; merry bells. Oh, glorious! Glorious!" Throughout the dreams Scrooge's mind has kept the real weather of the day on which he retired.

Part of the darkness motif is figured in the games hide-and-seek and blindman's-buff. It may be paraphrased as "none are so blind as those that will not see." Apparently in the recent past Scrooge has noticed the blind men's dogs pulling their masters from his path, and then wagging their tails as though they said, " 'No eye at all is better than an evil eye, dark master!' " The observation must have been Scrooge's. Perhaps, too, was the plight of his house, "up a yard, where it had so little business to be, that one could scarcely help fancying it must have run there when it was a young house, playing at hide-and-seek with other houses, and forgotten the way out again." Even Scrooge on this evening is being buffeted like a blind man in trying to find his house amid the fog and dark. His flight of fancy about the house ("one could scarcely help fancying it") must surely reflect his unformulated yet subconscious worry about his own state, which the personification of the lost house parallels. Whether Scrooge knew that Cratchit hurried home to play blindman's-buff we do not know, though his dreams and his Christmas actions in behalf of the Cratchits indicate that he knew a great deal about his clerk's family. In any case, in his dreams Scrooge imagines a game of blindman's-buff at his nephew's home, and he also imagines Martha Cratchit playing a game of hide-and-seek with her father. The blind men are buffeted out of love; their awakenings are joyous—in Scrooge's dreams, in his yearnings. It must be the case with Scrooge that he is lost yet struggling to be found.

BELLS AND HARDWARE

Cold, fog, and darkness afflict Scrooge's sight and feeling. The sound of bells also plagues him. It is significantly recurrent. At his counting-house it has long disturbed him: "The ancient tower of a church, whose gruff old bell was always peeping slyly down at Scrooge out of a Gothic window in the wall, became invisible, and struck the hours and quarters in the clouds, with tremendous vibrations afterward, as if its teeth were chattering in its frozen head up there." In his chambers, "his glance happened to rest upon a bell, a disused bell, that hung in the room, and communicated for some purpose now forgotten with a chamber in the highest story of the building." This is the bell that starts ringing mysteriously, then stops, and is followed by the clanking noise of Marley's ghost. This bell, as well as the others, symbolizes the mystery of what is lost to Scrooge—the proper use of time and service, of a call to human beings. Bells toll the coming of the spirits, though Scrooge's sense of time causes him to doubt their relevance ("The clock was wrong. An icicle must have got into the works.") Bells call happy people to church; they punctuate parties and other human assembly. At last Scrooge responds to bells without fear, but happily to "the lustiest peals he had ever heard." He has found the purpose for which the bell communicated with a chamber in the highest story of the building. He has had bells on his mind since the evening before, not merely because they marked time's passing but also because they connected people in warmth, worship, play, death, and love. This last would have a special tug upon Scrooge: the girl he was to have married long ago was named Belle.

The hardware of life haunts Scrooge, too—the forged metals which he has depended upon in place of human relations to secure, lock up, and insure what he will possess of existence. He has replaced with metal "solidity"; he has forged a chain, has relied on steel. But the hardware is unsubstantial. On Christmas Eve it melts into the hallucination of a doorknocker that comes alive in the likeness of Jacob Marley. And, though Scrooge doublelocks himself in, the hardware of Marley clanks to him, as does that of numerous other phantoms. Hardware reappears several times more as an undependable tool of life. The last of the Spirits takes Scrooge to a filthy den, a junk heap. "Upon the floor within, were piled up heaps of rusty keys, nails, chains, hinges, files, scales, weights, and refuse iron of all kinds. Secrets that few would like to scrutinise were bred and hidden in mountains of unseemly rags, masses of corrupted fat, and sepulchres of bones." It is here that the dreamed-of charwoman, laundress, and undertaker's man bring to sell for hard cash the only effects of dreamed-of dead Scrooge. And his imagined effects belong here, among the junk. For these, material possessions, Scrooge has traded human love. In the dreams his fear of losing them has emerged. Spirits from the outside world have come into Scrooge's counting-house this afternoon—his nephew, the charity gentlemen, the lad who sang through the keyhole:

> 'God bless you, merry gentleman!
> May nothing you dismay!'

They have asked for his money and love. Worse, they have threatened his only security: the belief in only material possession. In the dreams their invasion is reasserted by magnification into phantoms who would take away his wealth.

Selling Scrooge's possessions in the dream, the women say, " 'Who's the worse for the loss of a few things like these? Not a dead man, I suppose?' 'No, indeed,' said Mrs. Dilber, laughing. 'If he wanted to keep 'em after he was dead, a wicked old screw,' pursued the woman, 'why wasn't he natural in his lifetime?' " Scrooge, like an old screw—a piece of hardware himself—has not been natural. This he has known subconsciously. He is struggling through metaphor to make himself aware of it; for he is not yet, in spite of appearances, inhuman. He is not yet as dead as a door-nail, which, as Dickens observes at the outset, is considered "the deadest piece of ironmongery in the trade." It was what Marley was as dead as, but not Scrooge, thanks to his submerged conscience.

It is easy to see why several other motifs should run through Scrooge's dreams—the many references to death and burial, to the passage of time, to the poor, to persons unhappy alone and happy gathered together. They are life that Scrooge has tried not to live by.

THE MARRIAGE MOTIF

One motif, marriage, needs exploration, however. The Christmas Eve of the dreams was not only the seventh anniversary of Jacob Marley's death—of Scrooge's last connection with a true fellow misanthropist—but it was also the afternoon he had replied to his nephew's invitation to dinner by saying he would see the nephew in hell first, then had blurted out as rationale: " 'Why did you get married?' " Love, to Scrooge, was the only symptom nearer insanity than the wish for a merry Christmas. Scrooge had built a wall of scorn against happy married life, and in the dreams we see his return to the problem, before and after the wall was built. In Stave Two, Belle sums up the problem: " 'You fear the world too much,' she answered, gently. 'All your hopes have merged into the hope of being beyond the chance of its sordid reproach. I have seen your nobler aspirations fall off one by one, until the master-passion, Gain, engrosses you.' "

But why does gain obsess him? Why has he given up Belle for gold? And why does marriage appall him? The answers may be revealed in the dreams. Taken back to his solitary and unhappy days as a schoolboy, Scrooge sees his old imagined friends of those days, characters from *The Arabian Nights,* and he cries: " 'And the Sultan's groom turned upside down by the Genii; there he is upon his head! Serve him right. I'm glad of it. What business had *he* to be married to the Princess!' " The groom is not good enough to marry the Princess, for he is poor. In the next scene of the dream Scrooge appears as a boy left at school while his classmates have gone home on holiday. He is discovered by his sister Fan (later to become mother of Scrooge's nephew), who announces her errand to take Scrooge home:

'To bring you home, home, home!'

'Home, little Fan?' returned the boy.

'Yes!' said the child, brimful of glee. 'Home, for good and all. Home for ever and ever. Father is so much kinder than he used to be, that home's like Heaven! He spoke so gently to me one dear night when I was going to bed, that I was not afraid to ask him once more if you might come home; and he said Yes, you should; and sent me in a coach to bring you. And you're to be a man!' said the child, opening her eyes, 'and are never to come back here; but first, we're to be together all the Christmas long, and have the merriest time in all the world.'

We can conjecture the relationship between Scrooge and his father; surely the father had been a tyrant, and possibly he had shaped the ideal of marriage for his son. Or, if one guesses, perhaps the father's cruelty resulted from money worries so that Scrooge felt marriage was possible only if the husband were secure financially. This at least seems to have led to the rift between Scrooge and Belle, which could very well have stemmed from the example of Scrooge's father. The simple fictional childhood of *Arabian Nights* and *Robinson Crusoe* ("Poor Robinson Crusoe, where have you been, Robinson Crusoe?") has been lost, cut in upon by the harsh facts of economic life. Obsession with wealth for its own sake has begun as a desire to build a platform on which to base married life. The obsession has made love for anything but gold impossible. This is what ailed Scrooge—this and the submerged struggle against the master-passion, Gain at the expense of humanity and in the interest of dehumanization.

Scrooge has observed and evidently thought kindly upon the marriages of the Fezziwigs and Cratchits. But the former was overshadowed by fear of insecurity in marriage; Scrooge's youthful sympathy for the Fezziwigs' union was submerged. Similarly, Scrooge's reveling in the happy-and-threatened Cratchit family remained under his flinty consciousness until the dream conversion. Of his sister's marriage we learn only that it resulted in Fan's death; apparently Scrooge cannot think upon it further. He has believed the only safe road is the one to personal economic security. Travel along that road, as Scrooge takes it, necessitates avoidance of human love.

SCROOGE'S EPIPHANY

No change can come from without his mind. His emergence must originate in his mind, for that is where he has locked everything up. The dreams are remembrances and imaginings based on remembrance. They are subconscious fears. Moreover, they have been so tightly, inhumanly, pressed that they must burst forth, and Scrooge must either in his crisis reform totally or not at all. There is no degree of inhumanity. It is true that he overcompensates and becomes a ridiculous countercaricature. But then he has shocked himself severely. The understanding of self has been huge; so its early manifestations were bound to be foolish. If it is difficult to imagine such overnight conversion, it is even more difficult to imagine a gradual one. He is being smothered by his isolationist creed; so he must throw it off violently. Scrooge is either a human being and must understand it, or become a thing. On this fateful Christmas Eve he has denied all he has had of human life—family, friendship, love, charity—indeed, all fellow-feeling. He can no longer find life enough to breathe in isolation; he must break out into the world. The dreams—inner explosions of conscience—are the last resort.

They are not reform theory. They do not echo pamphlets, or legislation, or sermons from the public pulpit, but individual human conscience. They come from the effects of a lifetime at last asserted. Thus they can, apparently at a stroke, overset the habits of many misled years.

The Conversion of Scrooge

Joseph Gold

In his book *Charles Dickens: Radical Moralist,*
Joseph Gold argues that *A Christmas Carol* represents "the whole synthesis of Dickens's moral theory
at this point in his career," for Dickens is totally
committed to the subject of conversion. In his analysis of Scrooge's conversion, Gold points out that
Scrooge and his dead partner Marley are a single
entity—for a part of Scrooge is indeed dead. Further,
the visits from the three Christmas spirits are akin to
psychotherapy: Healing begins—and by extension
conversion—when the relentless ghosts force
Scrooge to witness repressed images from his past.

Written during the period of *Martin Chuzzlewit*'s composition, *A Christmas Carol* represents in a simple metaphor the
whole synthesis of Dickens' moral theory at this point in his
career. Scrooge, like Old Martin Chuzzlewit, is the subject of
conversion. It is true that conversion here is not much more
than magical or symbolic. Indeed, by writing a fairy or ghost
tale, Dickens deliberately avoids dealing with the question of
psychological or spiritual growth. Nevertheless it is of para-
mount importance to an understanding of all Dickens' work
to realize that he has settled on and clearly delineated his
subject as conversion. As [Edgar] Johnson points out, in his
brilliant essay on this novel, "Scrooge's conversion is more
than the transformation of a single human being. It is a plea
for society itself to undergo a change of heart." Dickens has
flirted with the conversion idea before in all his writing.
Oliver pleads with Fagin and Nancy pleads with Sikes for
conversion. Nicholas and Old Man Trent, the two Martins
and Mrs. Varden are all subject to this moral pressure by
their creator. Only now, however, do we see how clearly and
totally is Dickens committed to this view.

Excerpted from *Charles Dickens: Radical Moralist,* by Joseph Gold (Minneapolis: University of Minnesota Press, 1972). Reprinted with permission from the author.

Converted from what to what? *A Christmas Carol* gives the answer more precisely and more simply than anywhere else in Dickens—converted from closedness to openness, from frigidity to warmth, from isolation to brotherhood, from death to life. This is the meaning of Scrooge and Marley and this is the meaning of Christmas. [As Johnson writes:]

Dickens is certain that the enjoyment most men are able to feel in the happiness of others can play a larger part than it does in the tenor of their lives. The sense of brotherhood, he feels, can be broadened to a deeper and more active concern for the welfare of all mankind. It is in this light that Dickens sees the Spirit of Christmas. So understood, as the distinguished scholar Professor Louis Cazamian rightly points out, his "philosophie de Noël" becomes the very core of his social thinking.

Christmas comes to represent the recurring possibility, the residual touchstone event of time that symbolically offers us the evidence and experience of brotherhood and openness. It is Christmas all the time for the annual event is only ritual expression of ever-present spiritual possibility. Christmas takes place in the mind and the mind of the individual, Scrooge's mind, is Dickens' vehicle for his presentation of the Christmas Spirit.

THE ROLE OF MARLEY

Scrooge and Marley are one and the same. Dickens loves to see the inherent ironies in business forms or idioms of language and just as he plays with the idea of the firm's name, Dombey and Son, so he presents "Scrooge and Marley" as a single entity.

Scrooge never painted out Old Marley's name. There it stood, years afterwards, above the warehouse door: Scrooge and Marley.

Marley is now dead and Dickens tells us how important it is for us to understand that fact: "There is no doubt that Marley was dead. This must be distinctly understood, or nothing wonderful can come of the story I am going to relate." If Hamlet's father had not been dead, Dickens tells us, the return of the ghost would lose its point. *Hamlet* also is a play about conversion and the allusion reinforces Dickens' subject—spiritual development and change initiated by confrontation with the past in the form of a ghost. Marley is dead as a "door-nail," which leads us smoothly to the door-knocker that becomes Marley himself. The door-knocker is the symbol of entrance, the link between cold outer world and domestic warmth. In view of Marley's subsequent rôle as the means by which Scrooge enters a new world it is entirely appropriate that he should first appear as a door-knocker. If Marley and Scrooge are one, or parts of the same, then Marley's being dead would suggest that part of Scrooge is dead. Scrooge does not, of course, know that he is dead. He thinks that life in others, his nephew for instance, is humbug, that is, pretense, cant, or delusion. Marley only discovered he had been dead in life after he was dead in death. The chains that Marley forged in life, the cash boxes that signify his spiritual bondage, he wears in death also, the only distinction being that now he knows he is chained. Scrooge is an old man and he sees Marley's ghost at Christmas and only after his interviews with his nephew and the collectors for charity. What happens subsequently suggests that Scrooge is not left undisturbed by these interviews. If Marley is part of Scrooge (or an image of him) and with his haunting brings Scrooge's past, present and future, it is not unreasonable to suppose that Scrooge is deeply troubled by his present life and wishes to alter his kinship to the Marley part of himself. It should be remembered that once there had been a Scrooge whom Scrooge wishes to become again. In other words, if the Marley of Marley-Scrooge can be laid to rest, Scrooge may be himself, which he is in the end, when he can say " 'I'm quite a baby.' " Scrooge finds that he is looking at himself in Marley. Of the chain Marley says " 'Is its pattern strange to *you*?' " and "Scrooge glanced about him on the floor, in the expectation of finding himself surrounded by some fifty or sixty fathoms of iron cable: but he could see nothing." It is only later that he comes to see everything. Chains and locks play an important part in *A Christmas Carol*. Scrooge lives in solitary confinement. He is "self-contained" and "solitary as an oyster." Like chains being dragged or unused doors which open reluctantly, he has a "grating voice." Even this changes, as we shall see. Scrooge imprisons himself: "Quite satisfied, he closed his door, and locked himself in; double-locked himself in, which was not his custom. Thus secured against surprise, he took off his cravat; . . ." He is attempting to lock out both his superstitious fear and Christmas itself. For Scrooge, Christmas is a particular trial and challenge. Christmas is seen by Dickens as a time

> . . . in the long calendar of the year, when men and women
> seem by one consent to open their shut-up hearts freely, and
> to think of people below them as if they really were fellow-
> passengers to the grave, and not another race of creatures
> bound on other journeys.

To Scrooge who shuns openness and contact and love it is
therefore a time for being particularly careful to shut himself away. " 'I wish to be left alone' said Scrooge." The wearing of chains, a practice which seems antithetical to Christmas, is widespread as Scrooge sees when he looks at the
many spirits flying round his house. "Every one of them
wore chains like Marley's Ghost; some few (they might be
guilty governments) were linked together; none were free."

Scrooge, "captive, bound, and double-ironed," sets about
the task of freeing himself with the assistance of three time
elements, the past, the present and the future. Up to this
point, Scrooge has been dead to all three. He cannot remember the past, yet it is remembered easily once the
process starts.

> "Remember it!" cried Scrooge with fervour; "I could walk it
> blindfold."
>
> "Strange to have forgotten it for so many years!" observed the
> Ghost. "Let us go on."

He does not live in the present—" 'It's not my business,' " and
he has no thought for the future, " 'Tell me what man that
was whom we saw lying dead?' " Scrooge must arrive at the
point where he can say " 'I will live in the Past, the Present,
and the Future.' " How may this be done?

PSYCHOTHERAPY

The rôles of Marley, former partner, and of the three Christmas spirits seem naturally to us now to fall into the mode of
psychotherapy and this is how the metaphor may make
sense to the reader of today. In a perfectly regular pattern the
therapy begins with the past and moves to the future. All
through the process violent change and discomfort are experienced by the presentation of images of the subject to
himself. Scrooge is taken back to his childhood and the be-
ginnings of his compassion start with pity for the image of
himself as a child. Only by self-compassion and self-
forgiveness are we led to relations with others in whom we
see ourselves. When Scrooge is asked by his first "guide"
what bothers him he replies " 'Nothing,' . . . 'Nothing.

There was a boy singing a Christmas Carol at my door last night. I should like to have given him something: that's all.' "
The situation of Scrooge and the first Spirit reads strangely like an account of modern therapy, as the patient is forced to witness, with undisguised agony, the repressed images of a rejected past.

> "Spirit?" said Scrooge, "show me no more! Conduct me home. Why do you delight to torture me?"
>
> "One shadow more!" exclaimed the Ghost.
>
> "No more!" cried Scrooge. "No more. I don't wish to see it. Show me no more!"
>
> But the relentless Ghost pinioned him in both his arms, and forced him to observe what happened next.

The girlfriend, who knew Scrooge much better than he knew himself, predicted that Scrooge would wipe out the memory of her. She even knew why Scrooge gave her up. " 'You fear the world too much,' she answered, gently." It is fear then that has made Scrooge close himself off, fear of the suffering and change that is life itself. From this point of view one might regard *A Christmas Carol,* in spite of all its supernatural imagery and religious overtones, as the most existential of parables. No wonder that many contemporary religionists regarded Dickens as a pagan thinker, for his love of holly and mistletoe and hot punch is one with his belief in immediate sensual, earthly rewards of spiritual conversion and brotherly love. Dickens continually reshapes Christian terms into a humanist mythology.

A knowledge of the past produces remorse and perhaps self-pity and a more general awareness of the self, but it is not enough. Understanding, hope, faith and love must be added to produce the second element of the courage to be. Scrooge must confront the general social consequences of his personal (and representative) frigid imprisonment. On two occasions the Spirit of Christmas Present quotes Scrooge's own words back at him. Scrooge has taken refuge in the present behind a shield of cant. " 'Man,' said the Ghost, 'if man you be in heart, not adamant, forbear that wicked cant until you have discovered What the surplus is, and Where it is.' " When he sees Ignorance and Want, that powerful piece of allegory of the boy and girl who will generate together the destruction of man and the world, he is again forced to hear his own words " 'Are there no prisons? Are there no workhouses?' " Scrooge must learn to look

upon Cratchit, not as a unit of economy, whose private circumstances are, for his employer, a happily-kept secret, but
as a human being who does not cease to be human because
he comes to work for Scrooge. When Scrooge sees the first
Spirit his bed-curtains have to be torn aside for him. When
the second Spirit comes Scrooge opens his curtains himself.
For the last Spirit Scrooge does not even have to return to his
bed, his therapist's couch. He meets it out in the world.
There remains only one element wanting to complete his
awakening.

The overriding image of the chapter "Last of the Spirits"
is that of death itself. What gives point to the life of compassion is the recognition that we are all "fellow passengers to
the grave." After the fact of our birth, the inevitability of our
death is what binds us together.

The Ghost of Christmas Past

*Roger Rosenblatt discusses the prominent role of the Ghost
of Christmas Past—and the importance of Scrooge's reaction to seeing himself as a lonely schoolboy.*

Dickens made us think that the third ghost did the trick, but I
believe it was the first. Naturally Scrooge was terrified by the
image of his future death, just as he was mortified by the
promise of its anonymity; after a night of whooping and rat-
tling he was ready to swear to anything; and the prognosis for
Tiny Tim undoubtedly touched his heart. Still, what really
turned the tide, I think, was the first vision conjured by the
Ghost of Christmas Past, the one of Scrooge as a boy sitting at
his desk in the near-deserted school at Christmas time. That
was Scrooge as we'd hardly known him, as he hardly knew
himself, no less lonely than the man he grew into, and certainly no happier; only young.

Christmas Past is the least picturesque of Dickens' spirits. It
has none of the fierce boisterousness of the Ghost of Christmas Present, none of the grey dreadfulness of the Ghost of
Christmas Yet to Come. A prosaic bear-but-a-touch-of-my-
hand ghost, it displays its episodes to Scrooge like a conventional historian, altering nothing, almost never stating the
morals of the tales, or recriminations. The past has already
happened, so what can a guide say but "there"? And it's a gentle ghost, besides; it doesn't overact like Marley.

Nevertheless it is "a strange figure" that parts Scrooge's bed
curtains: "like a child; yet not so like a child as like an old

Oh cold, cold, rigid, dreadful Death, set up thine altar here, and dress it with such terrors as thou hast at thy command: for this is thy dominion! But of the loved, revered, and honoured head, thou canst not turn one hair to thy dread purposes, or make one feature odious. It is not that the hand is heavy and will fall down when released; it is not that the heart and pulse are still; but that the hand WAS open, generous, and true; the heart brave, warm, and tender; and the pulse a man's. Strike, Shadow, strike! And see his good deeds springing from the wound, to sow the world with life immortal!

Scrooge must confront his own mortality. His great difficulty in recognizing his own death is his fear of stripping off the final veil, his last refuge from life. Everyone will die but Scrooge. If Scrooge cannot die, then it matters not what he does in life. But the Ghost is "relentless" and pulls back the

man, viewed through some supernatural medium, which gave him the appearance of having receded from the view, and being diminished to a child's proportions." The ghost embodies time. It knows, as Scrooge learns, that the past is as mysterious as the future, just as out of reach, as imprecise and malleable as the present, and as likely to be falsely seen or spoken for. The past is as wide open as the future too. When the ghost shows young Scrooge to the old it has had to choose carefully. All that immense and jumbled time in the old man's life, but only certain things will affect him. The boy at the desk is the first thing Scrooge sees on his journey, and he is immediately moved to tears. . . .

A hurt and lonely child is hard enough to bear, much less when that child is you, before the fall. You want back everything you were, and there you are: able to be hurt, unable to hurt back, unencumbered by your own ill will. As superintendent of such scenes, the Ghost of Christmas Past doesn't need to hoot and holler; there's terror enough in the act—to hurl back all those years and be the future gaping at the past as if it were bright as the future.

This is happening in Scrooge's mind: both the boy at school, and Scrooge looking at the boy. The man reaches for the child and vice versa, though they are reaching for two different things—Scrooge wishing to be young, but not lonely; the child wanting to be old, but not Scrooge. Neither will have it his way, yet Scrooge weeps "to see his poor forgotten self as it used to be."

Roger Rosenblatt, "*A Christmas Carol*," *The New Republic*, December 27, 1975.

unspeakable shroud that covers one's own face. Scrooge can come alive only when he sees that he is dead. How, Scrooge asks, can he "have his fate reversed?" His desperate appeal that it should be reversed is its reversion. Scrooge is a new man already.

SCROOGE'S TRANSFORMATION

When Scrooge is reborn he is the centre of all time, he lives in eternity for he is no longer the prisoner of time. " 'I will live in the Past, the Present, and the Future!' " His tears and his laughter are now free and so is his imagination. Now he can see what was invisible before.

> He went to church, and walked about the streets, and watched the people hurrying to and fro, and patted children on the head, and questioned beggars, and looked down into the kitchens of houses, and up to the windows, and found that everything could yield him pleasure. He had never dreamed that any walk—that anything—could give him so much happiness. In the afternoon he turned his steps towards his nephew's house.

The world is transformed precisely in proportion to the transformation of Scrooge's perception. It is the same world, but it is completely different also. Even Scrooge's grating voice is now altered: " 'Hallo!' growled Scrooge, in his accustomed voice, as near as he could feign it." *A Christmas Carol* begins with the knocker and ends with it. " 'I shall love it, as long as I live!' cried Scrooge, patting it with his hand. 'I scarcely ever looked at it before.' " Now indeed the knocker will represent a link, not a barrier, between Scrooge and the world.

Scrooge has had two allies all along in his agony of isolation, repression and fear. His nephew, Fred, and Bob Cratchit represent the salving spirit of Christmas. They have never abandoned hope and faith. They have waited for Scrooge, never giving up, so that they provide a natural point of resort and friendship when Scrooge is ready for them. Their patience with the intolerable old miser is indeed superhuman, but Dickens, I suppose, is demanding a humanity much larger and stronger than we normally think possible. Any sensitive reader of Dickens will share the anger and understand the irony expressed by Edgar Johnson at the end of the following quotation:

Dickens, however, leaves his surface action so entirely clear and the behavior of his characters so plain that they do not puzzle us into groping for gnomic meanings. Scrooge is a miser, his nephew a warmhearted fellow, Bob Cratchit a poor clerk—what could be simpler? If there is a touch of oddity in the details, that is merely Dickens's well-known comic grotesquerie; if Scrooge's change of heart is sharp and antithetical, that is only Dickens's melodramatic sentimentality. Surely all the world knows that Dickens is never profound?

Dickens is so profoundly radical perhaps that readers have preferred not to notice the challenges to our humanity in his work. His is above all a humanistic vision." [As Johnson notes] "What Dickens has at heart is not any economic conception like Marx's labor theory of value, but a feeling of the human value of human beings." The prisons and workhouses are made in the mind of Scrooge and only there will they be unmade. As far as Scrooge is concerned, the ghost of Marley is now laid to rest forever, for Jacob turns out to be a dear and living friend after all, and like his Biblical namesake, he has brought a ladder, up which Scrooge may climb to Heaven. In terms of the moral of Scrooge's own conversion Marley is saved as he saves Scrooge, for he comes alive in Scrooge's grateful memory. Scrooge's mind is the burial place and the resurrection place for Marley and the only possible place for such events. Dickens can now move on to a book-length story of conversion of a scope and insight not before attempted in the English novel. The move from the warehouse of "Scrooge and Marley" to the firm of "Dombey and Son" is a smooth and natural one.

CHAPTER 3

A Christmas Carol: Dickens's Christmas Vision

READINGS ON
A CHRISTMAS CAROL

Dickens's Exaltation of Christmas and Home

Catherine Waters

Catherine Waters writes that *A Christmas Carol* celebrates the realm of Christmas feeling that transcends
politics and class and is available to everyone. Specifically, the *Carol* portrays Dickens's exaltation of the
family and hearth, a vision inseparable from his social purpose. The Cratchit Christmas dinner, for example, exemplifies Dickens's ideal of domestic
harmony—a loving family set by a roaring fire in a
humble but snug home. Dickens bolsters this image
of rosy fireside comfort by contrasting it with the
wintry chill and darkness of outdoors. Ultimately,
through Scrooge's individual salvation—his conversion to the values of domesticity—Dickens advocates
the spread of Christmas and familial values throughout the social world. The following essay is excerpted from Waters's book *Dickens and the Politics
of the Family.*

The status of the *Carol* as a national institution in part ac-
counts for the nature of the critical response evident in early
reviews of the book as well as in later scholarship: the view
that the *Carol* transcends literary criticism, or is in some
way an inappropriate text for such analysis. [William Make-
peace] Thackeray's dismissal of 'objections regarding such a
book as this' in his February 1844 review for *Fraser's Magazine* set aside the criticisms he imagined the *Quarterly*'s reviewer making, and complemented the remarks of Laman
Blanchard in *Ainsworth's Magazine* that the *Carol* was a
book 'not to be talked or written of by ordinary rules'. Similarly, [biographer John] Forster concluded his account of its
success with the claim: 'Literary criticism here is a second-
rate thing, and the reader may be spared such discoveries as

it might have made in regard to the *Christmas Carol*? Philip Collins has speculated that modern critics may 'have been put off by the *Carol*'s institutional status (one might as readily undertake a rhetorical analysis of the Lord's Prayer)'. Whatever the explanation, this critical reverence or reticence helps to sustain the illusion of transcendence that distinguishes the *Carol*'s celebration of Christmas and sanctification of the hearth. The *Carol* works by affirming the possibility of reaching a position beyond the realm of class and politics, since its vision of Christmas is presented as available to everyone. By situating the *Carol* in a privileged domain according to the universality of its Christmas spirit, these early reviewers sought to confirm its message of transcendence. However, the special status given to the *Carol* in such contemporary reviews depends upon an opposition between the domain of politics and the realm of Christmas feeling that itself reproduces the gendered division of spheres involved in the middle-class ideology of the family. In this way, the critical reception of the *Carol* has been implicated in the formation of the middle-class Christmas represented in the tale.

From its first appearance, the *Carol* occupied a special place in Victorian middle-class culture. It carried the symbolic weight of the Christmas festival, implicitly requiring those who would criticise it to find themselves in league with the unreformed Scrooge. Authorised thus by the Victorian celebration of Christmas, the book simultaneously helped to shape and promote the festival upon which its marketability rested. It inaugurated a new publishing genre, flooding the market with Christmas Books resembling Dickens's that were designed to cash in on the gift-giving rituals of the season. Its status as commodity was clearly a significant element in the mutually authorising relationship that developed between the *Carol* and the Victorian middle-class Christmas. But this relationship was also fostered by the representational practices Dickens employed. He devised a narrative which appeared to determine its own mode of consumption at the firesides of the nation, exploiting and affirming the consumer culture and domestic ideology of the developing middle-class institution as part of his tale.

FIRESIDE NARRATION

Together with the supernatural elements, worship of the family, and overt social purpose which characterise Dickens's Christmas Books, the intimacy of tone adopted by the narrator is a crucial defining feature. Michael Slater aptly describes the tone of the *Carol* as that of 'a jolly, kind-hearted, bachelor uncle, seated across the hearth from his hearers on some festive domestic occasion'. The unmarried status of the narrator is important, for it frees him to construct a surrogate family among his readers. The jocularity and immediacy of address in the novel's opening establish the voice of the bachelor uncle, whose palpable presence as storyteller is most clearly insisted upon when Scrooge is confronted by the first of the three spirits: 'The curtains of his bed were drawn aside; and Scrooge, starting up into a half-recumbent attitude, found himself face to face with the unearthly visitor who drew them: as close to it as I am now to you, and I am standing in the spirit at your elbow'. The impression of physical proximity presented here seeks to determine the *Carol*'s mode of consumption. In his effort to produce a sense of oral narration, Dickens constructs the scene of reading in which the book is meant to be enjoyed. *A Christmas Carol* speaks not only for, but *from* the hearth, situating the reader—and the listener—in a domestic context that is projected by the tone and facilitated by the length of the work. Dickens apparently stressed this sense of fireside narration even more explicitly at his public readings of the *Carol*, on one occasion assuring his audience that 'nothing would be more in accordance with his wishes than that they should all, for the next two hours, make themselves as much as possible like a group of friends, listening to a tale told by a winter fire'.

The scene of family reading, constructed by the mode of narration, accords with the supernatural element in the tale. According to Forster, in writing the Christmas Books Dickens was taking the 'fairy fancies' and 'old nursery tales' told to him during his childhood, and 'giving them a higher form'. The fairy-tale themes, happenings and techniques that dominate the *Carol* help to produce the storybook atmosphere and to evoke the nostalgia associated with memories of childhood reading. But the introduction of the supernatural element carries political significance as well. The use of the spirits to unsettle Scrooge and challenge his hard empiricism is part of a larger epistemological enquiry generated by the fragmented experience of urban life shown in the tale. The spirits show Scrooge the inadequacy of his

empirical attitude, pointing out the existence of a realm beyond the bounds of his immediate external experience.
However, the transcendence attributed to this supernatural
realm is secured by obscuring the class specificity of the
representation of Christmas and the family in the *Carol*.
Scrooge's temporary freedom from spatial and temporal
limitations enables him to see rural- and city-dwellers as
part of a larger human family that is united by the spirit of
Christmas. But it is precisely by managing to render its dis-
course invisible in this way that a class achieves hegemony.

A Christmas Carol charts Scrooge's conversion from a
selfish, hard-hearted and miserly businessman into a jolly,
charitable, surrogate father. The determination to keep
Christmas and the absorption into the family that mark his
transformation show the inseparability of Dickens's social
purpose from his exaltation of family love. His message is
the need for Christian *caritas*, for the spread of goodwill
amongst all men, so that social misery might be alleviated
by a national conversion to the Christmas spirit. Scrooge is
the archetypal miser when the story begins: 'Hard and sharp
as flint, from which no steel had ever struck out generous
fire; secret, and self-contained, and solitary as an oyster. The
cold within him froze his old features, nipped his pointed
nose, shrivelled his cheek, stiffened his gait; made his eyes
red, his thin lips blue; and spoke out shrewdly in his grating
voice'. His association with the cold is ideologically significant in relation to the opposition between indoors and outdoors through which the domestic ideal is so often constructed in Dickens's fiction, and the fact that he carries 'his
own low temperature always about with him' establishes an
ominous parallel with the appearance of Marley's ghost,
which is 'provided with an infernal atmosphere of its own'.
Scrooge's struggle to blame the arrival of this spectre upon
his own indigestion—'You may be an undigested bit of
beef'—signifies his exclusion from those convivial feasters
in Dickens's fiction (such as the members of the Pickwick
club) whose capacity for fellow-feeling is manifested
through the healthiness of their appetites. His choice of a 'little saucepan of gruel' for his supper is a reflection of his par-
simony, and contrasts sharply with the inexhaustible supply
of edibles described with such verbal extravagance and relish elsewhere in the *Carol*.

THE DICKENSIAN HOME

However, as Paul Davis has shown, for the *Carol*'s earliest
readers Scrooge was not the emotional centre of the tale.
They saw the Cratchit family as the heart of the book, and
dramatic adaptations during the Victorian period often as-
signed the lead role to Bob Cratchit rather than Ebenezer
Scrooge. The Cratchit Christmas dinner is the most celebrated of Dickens's domestic set-pieces, and contains all the
essential ingredients for a happy Dickensian home: a clean
snug house, a hot fire, good homely food and drink, a
bustling little woman superintending the household, and a
large number of obedient and well-washed children. The
presence of the crippled Tiny Tim adds an element of sentimentality to the description which helps to evoke the shared
emotional response in the audience that would unite them
in a community of feeling. The depiction of Tiny Tim elicits
the empathy amongst his readers that Dickens saw as essential to the Christmas spirit.

The Cratchits make the most of their limited resources,
Mrs Cratchit being 'dressed out but poorly in a twice-turned
gown, but brave in ribbons'. Like the meal itself, the narrative of their humble celebration is 'eked out' by the emphasis given to the delights of anticipation, to the glorious air of
expectancy which grips the members of the family as they
await the arrival of daughter Martha, father Bob (bearing
Tiny Tim) and of the goose 'in high procession'. All of this
excitement is quite mild, however, in comparison with the
suspense which is generated as Mrs Cratchit poises the knife
in readiness to carve the wonderful bird: '[Grace] was succeeded by a breathless pause, as Mrs Cratchit, looking
slowly along the carving-knife, prepared to plunge it in the
breast; but when she did, and when the long-expected gush
of stuffing issued forth, one murmur of delight arose all
round the board'. Similarly, much is made of the general
trepidation which attends the momentous serving of the
Christmas pudding, as the narrator assumes the perspective
of the eager diners, who are tantalised by the sounds and
smells proceeding from the kitchen which herald its
coming:

> Hallo! A great deal of steam! The pudding was out of the cop-
> per. A smell like a washing-day! That was the cloth. A smell

> like an eating-house and a pastrycook's next door to each
> other, with a laundress's next door to that! That was the pud-
> ding! In half a minute Mrs Cratchit entered—flushed, but
> smiling proudly—with the pudding, like a speckled cannon-
> ball, so hard and firm, blazing in half of half-a-quartern of
> ignited brandy, and bedight with Christmas holly stuck into
> the top.

The dinner over and the clean-up completed, all of the
Cratchit family draw together in a circle around the hearth.
As a reviewer of Dickens's fourth Christmas Book wryly
noted,

> we feel convinced, [that] had Italy, or Spain, or any country
> nearer the tropics than ours produced [Mr Dickens], instead
> of describing lazzaroni, and maccaroni, and water melons, or
> Andalusian young ladies, and cigaritos, and chocolate, and
> mantillas, he would have migrated to our more northern
> shores for the sake of firesides, purring cats, boiling kettles,
> Dutch clocks and chirping crickets.

In the *Carol,* the familial values of love, charity and good humour associated with the focus on the hearth are supple-
mented by the comfort and security of warm punch, compounded and dispensed by Bob, and crackling chestnuts.
Shared in a family circle, food and drink represent physical,
emotional and spiritual nourishment. . . .

All of the Christmas Books establish a woman's embodiment of the domestic ideal as the grounds for her sexual appeal to the male. Indeed, the avuncular narrator is frequently characterised through his adoption of a January-like
position with respect to the young women he describes, and
this disparity in age makes his delight in their rosy charms
more piquant. In the *Carol* the narrator describes Scrooge's
niece with an obvious relish for her childish appearance,
and in foretelling the fate of Scrooge's lost love he observes
her eldest daughter being 'pillaged' by the younger children
of the family, and envies their sport with a zeal that is un-
comfortably reminiscent of the lascivious Quilp. In [*The
Cricket on the Hearth*], it is Dot's small and childish stature
and 'chubby little hands' that elicit the narrator's admiration. He observes that she is 'something of what is called the
dumpling shape', adding, 'but I don't myself object to that'.
Dot is good enough to eat, and this association of female de-
sirability with food is entirely in keeping with the gastro-
nomic fervour of the Christmas Books, where everything is
edible and offers itself to be eaten with a liberality that tan-

talisingly suggests a kind of sexual freedom. In the *Carol* the narrator describes the 'Norfolk Biffins' at the fruiterer's shop: 'squab and swarthy, setting off the yellow of the oranges and lemons, and, in the great compactness of their juicy persons, urgently entreating and beseeching to be carried home in paper bags and eaten after dinner', and the French plums at the grocer's that 'blushed in modest tartness from their highly-decorated boxes'. In the representation of his anthropomorphic fruit and edible young women, Dickens domesticates the Saturnalian impulses traditionally associated with the Christmas season for a middle-class consumer culture.

INDOOR/OUTDOOR OPPOSITION

The potency of the domestic set-pieces, which centre on women like Dot Peerybingle in the Christmas Books, is enhanced by the contrast drawn between indoor and outdoor settings and by the manipulation of narrative perspective. . . .

The indoor/outdoor opposition . . . [is] a vital part of the exaltation of home in the *Carol*. The scene of the Cratchit dinner is presided over by the Ghost of Christmas Present, and Scrooge is a privileged and secret witness to the festivities taking place within the home. His hidden viewpoint emphasises the allure of the private family celebration. A similar effect is apparent in the narrator's description of the coming night:

> By this time it was getting dark, and snowing pretty heavily; and as Scrooge and the Spirit went along the streets, the brightness of the roaring fires in kitchens, parlours, and all sorts of rooms, was wonderful. Here, the flickering of the blaze showed preparations for a cosy dinner, with hot plates baking through and through before the fire, and deep red curtains, ready to be drawn to shut out cold and darkness.

It is the fleeting vision, the stolen glimpse of a cosy place of privacy, that produces the impact of these scenes. In each of the vignettes presented by the spirits, Scrooge is the unseen observer, the witness who is excluded from being a participant in the action. This narrative dependence upon voyeurism itself inscribes the opposition between warm inside and cold outside through which the ideal of domesticity is largely constituted. In *The Battle of Life*, this opposition is

invoked in the description of the day upon which Alfred
Heathfield is expected to return to his foster-family:

> A raging winter day, that shook the old house, sometimes, as
> if it shivered in the blast. A day to make home doubly home.
> To give the chimney-corner new delights. To shed a ruddier
> glow upon the faces gathered round the hearth, and draw
> each fireside group into a closer and more social league,
> against the roaring elements without. Such a wild winter day
> as best prepares the way for shut-out night; for curtained
> rooms, and cheerful looks; for music, laughter, dancing, light,
> and jovial entertainment!

The emphasis upon protection, enclosure and security, associated with the interior of the home, asserts the value of
privacy. This kind of spatial differentiation is also repro-
duced in the narrative frames of the *Carol* which position
Scrooge as the unseen viewer, and the recurrence of these
symbolic oppositions between inside and outside throughout the Christmas Books promotes the separation of public
and private spheres underpinning the ideal of domesticity.
The framing devices help to reproduce the boundaries con-
stituting middle-class ideology.

Dickens's choice of a businessman to embody his moral
in the *Carol* enables him to make social comments about
employer-employee relationships. But the significance of
this choice is not restricted to the provision of commentary
upon industrial relations. The unreformed Scrooge anticipates Mr Dombey in his failure to distinguish between his
personal and business life—between 'family' and 'firm'—
and his mistake is thus implicated in the definition of the domestic ideal. Scrooge lives in 'a gloomy suite of rooms, in a
lowering pile of building up a yard' which is 'old enough
now, and dreary enough, for nobody lived in it but Scrooge,
the other rooms being all let out as office'. Moreover, he be-
grudges his clerk the traditional holiday on Christmas Day,
deriding it as an excuse 'for picking a man's pocket every
twenty-fifth of December!'. And in seeking to do away with
the work/holiday distinction, he demonstrates his rejection
of middle-class family life.

SOCIAL REFORM

Scrooge's domestic salvation is meant to serve as an emblem
of social reform, the promise of a regenerated social system,
although the wish-fulfilment of this fictional strategy is evident. Whether or not the cheering prospect of a wholesale

change in human nature is convincingly represented, this substitution of individual moral transformation for social reform is, in itself, a politically significant gesture. It reaffirms the distinction between public and private realms, by translating social conflicts into personal problems that are solvable through an individual act of will. The sanctification of the home is reaffirmed in this provision of a private resolution to the wider social problems addressed in the narrative. The solution to social deprivation enjoined by Scrooge's moral transformation is a universal conversion to the values of the Victorian middle-class Christmas: the Christmas which celebrates the domestic ideal. Nina Auerbach has argued that 'Christmas in this tale means family, and society viewed as a family: Scrooge rejects not God incarnate but his own role as munificent father'. But a more discriminating analysis of the conceptualisation of the family in the tale reveals an important distinction in its cultural message. Scrooge is not converted to a paternalistic ideal so much as to the values of domesticity. Rather than representing the family as a hierarchical model *for* social relations, the *Carol* advocates the spread of private, familial feeling and the virtues of the hearth *throughout* the social world. Dickens is concerned to view society not as '*a* family', but as composed of 'families', so that the ideal of domesticity might be spread throughout the commonwealth. And to this end the *Carol* projects itself into the hearth-side family circles of its readers. It asks to be purchased and read as a ritualised element of the Christmas celebration it is concerned to portray. Thus, in the closing lines of the *Carol* Dickens extends the benediction of Tiny Tim to his readers: 'it was always said of [Scrooge], that he knew how to keep Christmas well, if any man alive possessed the knowledge. May that be truly said of us, and all of us! And so, as Tiny Tim observed, God bless Us, Every One!' Apparently breaching the boundary of the fiction, the narrator seeks to dissolve social differences in a moral vision which consolidates the middle class and generalises its values as available to everyone.

Dickens's Defense
of Christmas

G.K. Chesterton

With the publication of *A Christmas Carol*, Dickens
forever linked his name with the Christmas season.
In discussing the link between Dickens and Christmas, G.K. Chesterton identifies three qualities that
explain the Yuletide's unbreakable link with human
happiness and how Dickens integrated these elements into *A Christmas Carol*. G.K. Chesterton was a
British essayist, critic, novelist, and poet. In addition
to several collections of essays, Chesterton is the author of *Charles Dickens: The Last of the Great Men*
and *Appreciations and Criticisms of the Works of
Charles Dickens*, from which the following essay is
excerpted.

The mystery of Christmas is in a manner identical with the
mystery of Dickens. If ever we adequately explain the one we
may adequately explain the other. And indeed, in the treatment of the two, the chronological or historical order must
in some degree be remembered. Before we come to the
question of what Dickens did for Christmas we must consider the question of what Christmas did for Dickens. How
did it happen that this bustling, nineteenth-century man, full
of the almost cock-sure common-sense of the utilitarian and
liberal epoch, came to associate his name chiefly in literary
history with the perpetuation of a half pagan and half
Catholic festival which he would certainly have called an
antiquity and might easily have called a superstition? Christmas has indeed been celebrated before in English literature;
but it had, in the most noticeable cases, been celebrated in
connection with that kind of feudalism with which Dickens
would have severed his connection with an ignorant and
even excessive scorn. Sir Roger de Coverley kept Christmas;
but it was a feudal Christmas. Sir Walter Scott sang in praise

Excerpted from *Appreciations and Criticisms of the Works of Charles Dickens*, by G.K.
Chesterton. (New York: Dutton, 1911).

of Christmas; but it was a feudal Christmas. And Dickens was not only indifferent to the dignity of the old country gentleman or to the genial archæology of Scott; he was even harshly and insolently hostile to it. If Dickens had lived in the neighbourhood of Sir Roger de Coverley he would undoubtedly, like Tom Touchy, have been always "having the law of him." If Dickens had stumbled in among the old armour and quaint folios of Scott's study he would certainly have read his brother novelist a lesson in no measured terms about the futility of thus fumbling in the dust-bins of old oppression and error. So far from Dickens being one of those who like a thing because it is old, he was one of those cruder kind of reformers, in theory at least, who actually dislike a thing because it is old. He was not merely the more righteous kind of Radical who tries to uproot abuses; he was partly also that more suicidal kind of Radical who tries to uproot himself. In theory at any rate, he had no adequate conception of the importance of human tradition; in his time it had been twisted and falsified into the form of an opposition to democracy. In truth, of course, tradition is the most democratic of all things, for tradition is merely a democracy of the dead as well as the living. But Dickens and his special group or generation had no grasp of this permanent position; they had been called to a special war for the righting of special wrongs. In so far as such an institution as Christmas was old, Dickens would even have tended to despise it. He could never have put the matter to himself in the correct way—that while there are some things whose antiquity does prove that they are dying, there are some other things whose antiquity only proves that they cannot die. If some Radical contemporary and friend of Dickens had happened to say to him that in defending the mince-pies and the mummeries of Christmas he was defending a piece of barbaric and brutal ritualism, doomed to disappear in the light of reason along with the Boy-Bishop and the Lord of Misrule, I am not sure that Dickens (though he was one of the readiest and most rapid masters of reply in history) would have found it very easy upon his own principles to answer. It was by a great ancestral instinct that he defended Christmas; by that sacred sub-consciousness which is called tradition, which some have called a dead thing, but which is really a thing far more living than the intellect. There is a dark kinship and brotherhood of all mankind which is much too deep to be called heredity or to be in any way explained in scientific formulæ; blood is thicker than water and is especially very much thicker than water on the brain. But this unconscious and even automatic quality in Dickens's defence of the Christmas feast, this fact that his defence might almost be called animal rather than mental, though in proper language it should be called merely virile; all this brings us back to the fact that we must begin with the atmosphere of the subject itself. We must not ask Dickens what Christmas is, for with all his heat and eloquence he does not know. Rather we must ask Christmas what Dickens is—ask how this strange child of Christmas came to be born out of due time.

INDESCRIBABLE HAPPINESS

Dickens devoted his genius in a somewhat special sense to the description of happiness. No other literary man of his eminence has made this central human aim so specially his subject matter. Happiness is a mystery—generally a momentary mystery—which seldom stops long enough to submit itself to artistic observation, and which, even when it is habitual, has something about it which renders artistic description almost impossible. There are twenty tiny minor poets who can describe fairly impressively an eternity of agony; there are very few even of the eternal poets who can describe ten minutes of satisfaction. Nevertheless, mankind being half divine is always in love with the impossible, and numberless attempts have been made from the beginning of human literature to describe a real state of felicity. Upon the whole, I think, the most successful have been the most frankly physical and symbolic; the flowers of Eden or the jewels of the New Jerusalem. Many writers, for instance, have called the gold and chrysolite of the Holy City a vulgar lump of jewellery. But when these critics themselves attempt to describe their conceptions of future happiness, it is always some priggish nonsense about "planes," about "cycles of fulfilment," or "spirals of spiritual evolution." Now a cycle is just as much a physical metaphor as a flower of Eden; a spiral is just as much a physical metaphor as a precious stone. But, after all, a garden is a beautiful thing; whereas this is by no means necessarily true of a cycle, as can be seen in the case of a bicycle. A jewel, after all, is a beautiful thing; but this is not necessarily so of a spiral, as can be seen in the case of a corkscrew. Nothing is gained by dropping the old material metaphors, which did hint at heavenly beauty, and adopting other material metaphors which do not even give a hint of earthly beauty. This modern or spiral method of describing indescribable happiness may, I think, be dismissed. Then there has been another method which has been adopted by many men of a very real poetical genius. It was

THE VICTORIAN CAROL

Paul Davis comments on why A Christmas Carol *appealed so strongly to Dickens's contemporaries, who read the* Carol *as a retelling of the biblical Christmas story.*

For Dickens's contemporaries the *Carol* was a parable. It told the same popular tale that George Eliot would later tell in *Silas Marner*, the story of a miser who learns charity through the agency of a child. But more important in the 1840s, Dickens's story proved that urbanization had not destroyed Christmas. In the British imagination, Christmas was associated with the manor house, peasant revels, and baronial feasts. During the first half of the nineteenth century—particularly in the two decades that preceded the publication of the *Carol*—the growth of industry and cities threatened this rural holiday by threatening its country seat. Dickens's story provided celebratory proof that the old Christmas could flourish in the new cities, in spite of dour Dissenting tradesmen who condemned Christmas revels. Scrooge's reformation thus became urban Britain's counter-reformation to puritanical excess.

The Victorian *Carol* connected the city to the traditions of the country. It also revealed a new urban world infused with spirits and so it became a kind of scripture. As Darwinism and doubt undermined the authority of the Bible, secular texts that assumed biblical authority were especially valued. Although we now see the *Carol* as a secular book, later Victorians of the 1870s, the decade following Dickens's death, read his Christmas story as a retelling of the biblical Christmas story. Scrooge became a nineteenth-century pilgrim, a modern-day magus seeking the Christ child, while the Cratchits reenacted the holy family. For later Victorians the *Carol* was secular scripture.

Paul Davis, "Retelling *A Christmas Carol*: Text and Culture-Text," *The American Scholar*, Winter 1990.

the method of the old pastoral poets like Theocritus. It was in another way that adopted by the elegance and piety of Spenser. It was certainly expressed in the pictures of Watteau; and it had a very sympathetic and even manly expression in modern England in the decorative poetry of William Morris. These men of genius, from Theocritus to Morris, occupied themselves in endeavouring to describe happiness as a state of certain human beings, the atmosphere of a commonwealth, the enduring climate of certain cities or islands. They poured forth treasures of the truest kind of imagination upon describing the happy lives and landscapes of Utopia or Atlantis or the Earthly Paradise. They traced with the most tender accuracy the tracery of its fruit-trees or the glimmering garments of its women; they used every ingenuity of colour or intricate shape to suggest its infinite delight. And what they succeeded in suggesting was always its infinite melancholy. William Morris described the Earthly Paradise in such a way that the only strong emotional note left on the mind was the feeling of how homeless his travellers felt in that alien Elysium; and the reader sympathised with them, feeling that he would prefer not only Elizabethan England but even twentieth-century Camberwell to such a land of shining shadows. Thus literature has almost always failed in endeavouring to describe happiness as a state. Human tradition, human custom and folk-lore (though far more true and reliable than literature as a rule) have not often succeeded in giving quite the correct symbols for a real atmosphere of *camaraderie* and joy. But here and there the note has been struck with the sudden vibration of the *vox humana*. In human tradition it has been struck chiefly in the old celebrations of Christmas. In literature it has been struck chiefly in Dickens's Christmas tales.

In the historic celebration of Christmas as it remains from Catholic times in certain northern countries (and it is to be remembered that in Catholic times the northern countries were, if possible, more Catholic than anybody else), there are three qualities which explain, I think, its hold upon the human sense of happiness, especially in such men as Dickens. There are three notes of Christmas, so to speak, which are also notes of happiness, and which the pagans and the Utopians forget. If we state what they are in the case of Christmas, it will be quite sufficiently obvious how important they are in the case of Dickens.

DRAMA

The first quality is what may be called the dramatic quality. The happiness is not a state; it is a crisis. All the old customs surrounding the celebration of the birth of Christ are made by human instinct so as to insist and re-insist upon this crucial quality. Everything is so arranged that the whole household may feel, if possible, as a household does when a child is actually being born in it. The thing is a vigil and a vigil with a definite limit. People sit up at night until they hear the bells ring. Or they try to sleep at night in order to see their presents the next morning. Everywhere there is a limitation, a restraint; at one moment the door is shut, at the moment after it is opened. The hour has come or it has not come; the parcels are undone or they are not undone; there is no evolution of Christmas presents. This sharp and theatrical quality in pleasure, which human instinct and the mother wit of the world has wisely put into the popular celebrations of Christmas, is also a quality which is essential in such romantic literature as Dickens wrote. In romantic literature the hero and heroine must indeed be happy, but they must also be unexpectedly happy. This is the first connecting link between literature and the old religious feast; this is the first connecting link between Dickens and Christmas.

ANTAGONISM

The second element to be found in all such festivity and all such romance is the element which is represented as well as it could be represented by the mere fact that Christmas occurs in the winter. It is the element not merely of contrast, but actually of antagonism. It preserves everything that was best in the merely primitive or pagan view of such ceremonies or such banquets. If we are carousing, at least we are warriors carousing. We hang above us, as it were, the shields and battle-axes with which we must do battle with the giants of the snow and hail. All comfort must be based on discomfort. Man chooses when he wishes to be most joyful the very moment when the whole material universe is most sad. It is this contradiction and mystical defiance which gives a quality of manliness and reality to the old winter feasts which is not characteristic of the sunny felicities of the Earthly Paradise. And this curious element has been carried out even in all the trivial jokes and tasks that have always surrounded such occasions as these. The object of the jovial customs was not to make everything artificially easy: on the contrary, it was rather to make everything artificially difficult. Idealism is not only expressed by shooting an arrow at the stars; the fundamental principle of idealism is also expressed by putting a leg of mutton at the top of a greasy pole. There is in all such observances a quality which can be called only the quality of divine obstruction. For instance, in the game of snapdragon (that admirable occupation) the conception is that raisins taste much nicer if they are brands saved from the burning. About all Christmas things there is something a little nobler, if only nobler in form and theory, than mere comfort; even holly is prickly. It is not hard to see the connection of this kind of historic instinct with a romantic writer like Dickens. The healthy novelist must always play snapdragon with his principal characters; he must always be snatching the hero and heroine like raisins out of the fire.

THE GROTESQUE

The third great Christmas element is the element of the grotesque. The grotesque is the natural expression of joy; and all the Utopias and new Edens of the poets fail to give a real impression of enjoyment, very largely because they leave out the grotesque. A man in most modern Utopias cannot really be happy; he is too dignified. A man in Morris's Earthly Paradise cannot really be enjoying himself; he is too decorative. When real human beings have real delights they tend to express them entirely in grotesques—I might almost say entirely in goblins. On Christmas Eve one may talk about ghosts so long as they are turnip ghosts. But one would not be allowed (I hope, in any decent family) to talk on Christmas Eve about astral bodies. The boar's head of old Yuletime was as grotesque as the donkey's head of Bottom the Weaver. But there is only one set of goblins quite wild enough to express the wild goodwill of Christmas. Those goblins are the characters of Dickens.

Arcadian poets and Arcadian painters have striven to express happiness by means of beautiful figures. Dickens understood that happiness is best expressed by ugly figures. In beauty, perhaps, there is something allied to sadness; certainly there is something akin to joy in the grotesque, nay, in the uncouth. There is something mysteriously associated with happiness not only in the corpulence of Falstaff and the corpulence of Tony Weller, but even in the red nose of Bardolph or the red nose of Mr. Stiggins. A thing of beauty is an inspiration for ever—a matter of meditation for ever. It is rather a thing of ugliness that is strictly a joy for ever.

THE SUPERIORITY OF THE *CAROL*

All Dickens's books are Christmas books. But this is still truest of his two or three famous Yuletide tales—*The Christmas Carol* and *The Chimes* and *The Cricket on the Hearth*. Of these *The Christmas Carol* is beyond comparison the best as well as the most popular. Indeed, Dickens is in so profound and spiritual a sense a popular author that in his case, unlike most others, it can generally be said that the best work is the most popular. It is for *Pickwick* that he is best known; and upon the whole it is for *Pickwick* that he is best worth knowing. In any case this superiority of *The Christmas Carol* makes it convenient for us to take it as an example of the generalisations already made. If we study the very real atmosphere of rejoicing and of riotous charity in *The Christmas Carol* we shall find that all the three marks I have mentioned are unmistakably visible. *The Christmas Carol* is a happy story first, because it describes an abrupt and dramatic change. It is not only the story of a conversion, but of a sudden conversion; as sudden as the conversion of a man at a Salvation Army meeting. Popular religion is quite right in insisting on the fact of a crisis in most things. It is true that the man at the Salvation Army meeting would probably be converted from the punch bowl; whereas Scrooge was converted to it. That only means that Scrooge and Dickens represented a higher and more historic Christianity.

Again, *The Christmas Carol* owes much of its hilarity to our second source—the fact of its being a tale of winter and of a very wintry winter. There is much about comfort in the story; yet the comfort is never enervating: it is saved from that by a tingle of something bitter and bracing in the weather. Lastly, the story exemplifies throughout the power of the third principle—the kinship between gaiety and the grotesque. Everybody is happy because nobody is dignified. We have a feeling somehow that Scrooge looked even uglier when he was kind than he had looked when he was cruel. The turkey that Scrooge bought was so fat, says Dickens, that it could never have stood upright. That top-heavy and monstrous bird is a good symbol of the top-heavy happiness of the stories.

A Carol for Mankind

J.H. McNulty

J.H. McNulty calls *A Christmas Carol* "the one perfect short story Dickens wrote" and considers it the
best known book in the English language after the
Bible. In his tribute to the *Carol*, McNulty concludes
that the story is true to human experience. Thus, the
Carol is much more than a simple ghost story about
Scrooge's conversion; rather, it tells the story about
what happens to everyone at Christmastime. On
Christmas Eve, for example, all people are visited by
the Ghost of Christmas Past in the form of memories.
Likewise, the Ghost of Christmas Present reminds all
people that cheerfulness should be practiced at
Christmastime. McNulty has written several articles
on the literature of Charles Dickens.

A Christmas Carol stands out alone as the one perfect short
story Dickens wrote. We may say of it as Macaulay said of
"Boswell's Life of Johnson," "Eclipse is first and the rest
nowhere." Dickens's other Christmas stories have little more
to do with the festive season than "Winter's Tale" has to do
with winter, but this story is Christmas itself—Past, Present
and To Come. After the Bible it is the best-known book in the
language, and it has this unique distinction that if every copy
were destroyed to-day, it could be rewritten tomorrow, so
many know the story by heart. Even so, it may be possible to
say something about it which if not new, is at least not too
well known or stale.

LONDON FOG

It begins in a fog, not such a great fog as that with which
Bleak House opens, for that is probably the greatest fog in literature. All Londoners have a secret affection for fog. It is the
one thing London can, or at least could, produce to perfection. We cannot boast of our cloudless skies, they are too
rare, "like Angels' visits, few and far between"; nor of our

Reprinted from "Our Carol," by J.H. McNulty, *Dickensian*, vol. 34, 1937.

statues, they are often an insult to the memory of those in whose honour they are supposed to be erected; nor may we boast of our city churches, they are so frequently threatened with destruction, though the sentence has sometimes been deferred; nor of our ancient buildings, we destroy them as quickly as we can to make room for new ones.

But fog is ours. We loved it when we were young and when we discover that it has greater discomforts than pleasures we are on the verge of middle or old age. As Dickens never grew old we may well believe he never made that discovery.

The fogginess of Christmas Eve is used here for the sake of contrast to the "clear, bright, jovial, stirring cold" of Christmas Day, a day all blue and silver. There is a world of difference between the two days and the change from darkness to light, from fog to sunshine helps to show it. Then what a splendid background does the fog make to all Scrooge's visitors on that foggy afternoon.

How much more jolly and lively did Scrooge's nephew appear coming as he does out of the encircling gloom. How much more solid and benevolent did the portly gentlemen look emerging from the icy yellow mirk outside, even the voice of the carol singer at the keyhole might have sounded cheerful, if Scrooge had not silenced it, coming out of the surrounding darkness. Fog is the reverse of the Daylight Saving Act. It really does lessen the hours of daylight which the Act pretends to increase. Darkness, too, is necessary as a prelude to the appearance of Marley's Ghost. Shakespeare did a similar thing in *Macbeth* as a preparation for the dreadful vision of the dagger and the still more dreadful murder. It was night without moon or stars.

Banquo and Fleance and a servant with a torch are seen in a Court within the Castle.

BANQUO: How goes the night, boy?
FLEANCE: The moon is down; I have not heard the clock.
BANQUO: And she goes down at twelve.
FLEANCE: I take't, tis later, sir.
BANQUO: Hold take my sword: There's husbandry in heaven,
    Their candles are all out . . .

So it is here. Scrooge left his gloomy office, made his way through the dark, foggy streets, "dined at his usual melancholy tavern, and having read all the newspapers and beguiled the rest of the evening with his banker's book, went home to bed." He passed through the streets, now grown much darker, to his still more gloomy chambers where Marley, his deceased partner, had died seven years before on that very night. Here one must admire Scrooge's superb courage. As he paused before the street door, the knocker suddenly assumed the features of Marley; after a moment it resumed its original form. Scrooge entered the house, darker and more gloomy even than the street, and mounted the broad staircase. Again a horrid fancy assailed him that a hearse was going up before him: without a moment's hesitation he proceeded to his room and entered. Now Scrooge was not at his best to-night; he was suffering from a cold in his head—a most depressing malady, and was taking for it an even more depressing remedy—gruel. As he sat by the fire sipping this detestable beverage the bell in his room began to move slowly to and fro, then faster and then all the bells began ringing together.

There is nothing more unnerving than a bell that rings with no visible hand to ring it. When the sexton in *Barnaby Rudge* heard the ghostly bell toll before he touched his bell, he nearly fainted, rang his bell, how or how long he did not know, and ran home as fast as he could. Scrooge did not run away, he faced the music if you can call it such. Besides, where could he go? The office was closed, it was a bitter night, and there was nowhere else. He said, "Humbug."

The ringing was followed by the clanking of chains, footsteps on the stair, and the entrance of the terrible phantom. Scrooge seeing that the phantom was transparent, asked it to sit down, believing such an act to be impossible, and then there followed that excellent conversation which cannot be too much admired:

"You don't believe in me," observed the Ghost.

"I don't," said Scrooge.

"Why do you doubt your senses?"

"Because," said Scrooge, "a little thing affects them. A slight disorder of the stomach makes them cheats. You may be an undigested bit of beef, a blot of mustard, a crumb of cheese, a fragment of underdone potato. There's more of gravy than grave about you, whatever you are!"

· · · · ·

"I have but to swallow this (toothpick)," continued Scrooge, "and be for the rest of my days persecuted by a legion of goblins, all of my own creation. Humbug, I tell you—humbug!"

Compare this with another conversation with a ghost, that between Hamlet and his father's spirit.

While the spirit is present, Hamlet speaks to it with the deepest reverence, but the moment it disappears, talks of it as "True-penny," "Fellow in the cellarage," "Old Mole." This is indefensible.

With Scrooge it is quite a different matter. He and Marley had been partners and equals, whatever respect he had for Marley living he had none for his ghost, and in his pleasant sprightly conversation he showed it.

It was not till the ghost did that unpardonable thing, took off the bandage round its head and let its lower jaw drop on its breast that Scrooge's courage gave way and he fell upon his knees in terror; a man less brave than he would have been reduced to that state long before. Scrooge had not so many virtues that we should grudge him the possession of this one of courage.

It is not very astonishing that after his encounter with this horrible phantom he did not welcome the gift it promised him of a visit from three other spirits.

It is well known to all readers of Dickens that he is deeply moved, his prose becomes lyrical. Many passages in *The Old Curiosity Shop* and *A Tale of Two Cities* can, with the change of a word or two, become blank verse. It is, however, rather surprising that towards the end of his interview with Scrooge, Marley's ghost speaks in verse and utters the two most beautiful lines of verse that Dickens ever wrote.

"At this time of the rolling year," the spectre said, "I suffer most. Why did I walk through crowds of fellow beings with my eyes turned down,

And never raised them to that blessed Star
Which led the Wise Men to a poor abode."

After the prelude comes the *Carol* proper. One of its chief beauties is that it is essentially a true story. It is our carol, not merely the story of Scrooge's conversion but of Everyman's experience. What happened to Scrooge does happen to us. Many of us have known or have been Bob Cratchits, receiving from the Scrooges of our days the modern equivalent of fifteen shillings a week. We all know, or can easily find, plenty of Tiny Tims, many of whom unfortunately do die.

THE GHOST OF CHRISTMAS PAST

The Three Spirits also visit us. On Christmas Eve, the Ghost of Christmas Past appears. He comes laden with memories sad or bright and often bright with tears.

> "Then the forms of the departed
>   Enter at the open door;
> The beloved, the true-hearted,
>   Come to visit us once more:"

He bears a lamp, the Lamp of Memory, and the light of other days. The light may be dimmed or the memory dulled, but it is never quenched; "though Scrooge pressed it (the extinguisher) down with all his force, he could not hide the light." This Spirit, brings us memories of all the Golden Christmases of the Past.

He is aged "like an old man" for he is nearly 2,000 years old. Yet he has the face of a child without a wrinkle, for Christmas is the children's Feast and is always young and fresh. He bears a branch of holly, the most cheerful of evergreens, for Christmas is evergreen and unfading, and his dress is trimmed with summer flowers, for Christmas is the summer-time of the heart.

THE GHOST OF CHRISTMAS PRESENT

The Ghost of Christmas Present is a cheerful spirit and insists on us being the same. He reminds us that cheerfulness is a virtue, and though sometimes as difficult to practise as any other, one that should be particularly practised at Christmas-time. The visit of his elder brother may have left us sad, but he will take no denial. If we plead that our hearts are heavier and our pockets lighter than in past years and that we have little indeed to make us cheerful, he will show us, as he did Scrooge, many others who are in a far worse plight than we are, and have far less to make them happy than we have, yet who manage to preserve a cheerful face and light heart in their struggle with misfortune. He tells us that spiritual healing differs from physical, that here you bind up another's wounds in order to heal your own, and that the easiest way of becoming happy is to make others so.

Dickens has beautifully distinguished between the methods of approach of these Two Spirits. The Ghost of Christmas Past comes to Scrooge whether he will or no, and compels him to visit the scenes of his former life. He objects, but the Spirit insists. The Ghost of Christmas Present does not appear at all. Scrooge discovers his presence by the light streaming from the adjoining room and goes out to meet him. So it is with us. Memories of the Past will come to us on Christmas Eve whether we wish it or not. No door is stout enough to shut them out, but we can if we choose close our hearts against the duties of Christmas Present, though if we are wise we shall, like Scrooge, go to meet and welcome him.

THE GHOST OF CHRISTMAS YET TO COME

Like Scrooge, too, we must view with apprehension the approach of the Ghost of Christmas Yet to Come, that "solemn Phantom draped and hooded." Silence is the most terrible of his attributes and to us, also, the Future is silent, silent as the grave.

Do what we may we cannot help fearing his approach. We can, however, rob him of much of his horror by treating his two elder brothers well, and then he may turn out to be nothing more terrible than a bedpost, "and the bedpost was Scrooge's own."

He is the only one of the Spirits to be explained away as in a common Ghost Story. So Scrooge awakes, and so do we, to find that, Christmas Present is still with us and the gloomy phantom not yet on the horizon.

The Carol is a true story and we may be sometimes tempted to do with it what others have done elsewhere with other true stories. Just as historians have occasionally written History with an If: What would have happened *if* Napoleon had won the Battle of Waterloo? or what would be the state of England *if* the General Strike had succeeded? so we may ask what sort of a *Carol* should we have *if* Scrooge had died before Marley? or how did Scrooge spend the Christmas Day after his dream?

We know he had difficulty in dressing as he kept running about his room all the time, that shaving was not an easy matter for his hand was shaky. In the afternoon he went to his nephew's, but how did he spend his time there? The book does not tell us, but we can guess. How could any kindhearted man, and Scrooge was now a reformed character, go to a Christmas Party and keep that wonderful story to himself? Of course he told it. After dinner they would gather round the fire while Scrooge spoke of his wonderful dream. How they would shudder and look apprehensively at the dark corners of the room as Scrooge described the awful phantom, Marley's ghost. How they would shed a silent fear with the coming of the Ghost of Christmas Past and then brighten up at the approach of the cheerful spirit of Christmas Present. A slight shiver of apprehension would go round the circle as the Last of the Spirits made his appearance, and then Scrooge would cry, "What do you think he was, my dears? A bedpost, my own bedpost, and here I am to tell the tale."

Next day over a Christmas bowl of smoking bishop he would tell Bob Cratchit the story, and go home with him to finish that gigantic turkey which even the voracious young Cratchits could never have eaten in one day. These are the people who, we may imagine, would hear that story first which now the whole world has heard and applauded. The one short story which can take its place among the great novels. There it stands like a pigmy amongst giants, the Tiny Tim of the Dickens family who does not die; a very little volume—but a nugget of gold is always small; a good Englishman's version of the Angels' Song.

This is the book that has ensured a favourable answer to the prayer of another story, "Lord keep my memory green." It has done more than any other to keep his memory green, an evergreen which like the Holy Thorn of Glastonbury blossoms at Christmas-time, and by linking his name with that of Christmas has given him a share in the immortality of the immortal festival.

> How bright the little volume shines and glows
> Like holly berries mid the winter snows,
> Telling its tale as fragrant as the rose.
>
> Ever at Christmas-time it re-appears,
> Filling the hour with laughter and with tears,
> Recalling memories of vanished years.
>
> While from *The Carol's* music which now rings
> Throughout the world, giving to Hope new wings,
> We learn the loveliness of little things.
>
> Little and great; for as the rising sun
> Gives the glad tidings, "Christmas Day's begun"
> *The Carol* ends, "God bless us everyone."

A Christmas Carol Is a Superficial Crowd-Pleaser

D.B. Wyndham

A Christmas Carol celebrates Scrooge's redemption—
and how Christmas influences his conversion. Because Christmas is the spiritual center of the story,
D.B. Wyndham finds it remarkable that the *Carol* is
totally bereft of religious references. Wyndham attributes this paucity to Dickens's own doubts about
religion. In stripping Christmas of religion, Wyndham concludes, Dickens ultimately turned the holiday into a "joyless, meaningless, and boring orgy of
boozing and overeating." The following essay originally appeared in *The Universe*, a London
publication.

Reviewing the latest book on Charles Dickens, a critic raised
and answered an interesting question. What would have
happened if Dickens had joined the stream of converts who
followed Newman into the Church in the 1840–50's?

To which the answer was immediate. Since conversion
would have deprived Dickens automatically of his adoring
and enormous public, such a supposition is, humanly
speaking, what platform-bores call "beyond the sphere of
practical politics."

However, the theme makes a fascinating new toy for
Dickens-lovers, among whom I passionately count myself.

DICKENS AND CATHOLICISM

The master's attitude to the Oxford Movement I cannot discover, but his attitude to Catholicism is no mystery. Like
most healthy-minded Englishmen of his time, and many of
ours, he despised and detested it on principle from the cra-
dle. The most harmless priests he saw in Italy seemed to

Excerpted from "The Challenge of the Crib," by D.B. Wyndham, *The Universe*, December 9, 1949.

Autobiographical Details in *A Christmas Carol*
by Willoughby Matchett

It will be remembered that Bob Cratchit in the *Christmas Carol* lives in Camden Town. No one has ever located the house, but I fancy we shall not be far wrong in thinking that Dickens in dealing with it was drawing on his recollections of the Bayham Street life. His description of the Cratchit home as "four-roomed" is merely generic: one doubts if he actually visualised any special four-roomed house, although no doubt such houses were known to him: one doubts it because there are no descriptive details, and all the salient points of the house referred to casually are to be found in his own home. As a matter of fact, apart from basement, garret, and outhouses, this Bayham Street house is a four-roomed one. In itself the front parlour is just such a room as we can imagine the scene of the Cratchits' Christmas dinner: here is just such a closet door in it as that behind which Martha hides herself before Bob comes in with Tiny Tim. In the yard at the back we find a washhouse with a copper in it, and here we can well imagine the wonderful pudding being boiled. But a stronger reason for identifying the Cratchit home with Dickens's recollections of his own is this: the Cratchits are really the Dickenses in disguise.

"We were now six in all," Dickens told [biographer John] Forster, speaking of his brothers and sisters and himself at this Bayham Street period. So are the young Cratchits six. Moreover, they correspond exactly with the young Dickenses, with the exception that they are relatively all perhaps a little older. Martha, the eldest Cratchit, corresponds with Fanny, the eldest Dickens; Peter, the second Cratchit, with Charles himself; Belinda Cratchit with Letitia Dickens; an unnamed pair of Cratchits, boy and girl, with Frederick and Harriet Dickens; and finally we have Tiny Tim corresponding with Alfred, the Dickens baby of the time. That the young Dickenses could not have been six in number very long cannot be gainsaid, for the little girl Harriet died soon after the Chatham period, but, presumably, if the novelist was correct, not till after the family had left Bayham Street. David Copperfield, wearing crape round his much-worn little white hat for his mother, was probably taken from Charles's wearing such a sign of mourning for this little sister.

Willoughby Matchett, "Dickens in Bayham Street," *The Dickensian*, Vol. 5, 1970.

Dickens repulsive ogres (how amusing to think that he may more than once have passed that great, joyous servant of God, St. John Bosco, in the streets of Turin during his visit of 1853, and shuddered).

Though dazzled by the "flash and glory" of Italian basilicas, Dickens knew nothing of the Presence they contained—nor, less excusably, did young Mr. Newman, the Oxford intellectual, on his first Italian trip—and he deemed the Church everywhere on the continent to be obviously moribund. In a word, his impressions of the Catholicism of his own time were as babyish ([G.K.] Chesterton) as his impressions of the Middle Ages, which spelt to him nothing but tournaments and torture.

Chesterton, who loved him fervently, goes to the point—almost—with his usual swiftness in that brilliant little study *The Victorian Age in Literature*.

"When we think of the uncountable riches of religious art, imagery, ritual and popular legend that have clustered round Christmas through all the Christian ages, it is truly an extraordinary thing to reflect that Dickens (wishing to have in *A Christmas Carol* a little happy supernaturalism by the way of a change) actually had to make up a mythology for himself."

Even more curious—and a point overlooked by [G.K. Chesterton], not yet a Catholic—is the fact that although the theme of the book is the redemption of Scrooge by the influence of Christmas, the Incarnation—apart from a passing reference to "the veneration due to its [Christmas's] sacred name and origin," which may mean much or little—is not mentioned at all. . . .

A man writing a Christmas story is not bound to make a theological treatise of it, admittedly; but for a man using the Feast of Christmas as the spiritual pivot of his story to avoid all reference to its *raison d'être* seems to me a remarkable feat, and one which makes all the jovial uproar of the *Carol* sound oddly hollow.

No doubt the explanation is that Dickens, himself a kind of sentimental Unitarian (see his posthumous *Life of Our Lord*, and his own declaration in 1842), wisely evaded the challenge of God's Crib because he had his doubts about it. . . .

At any rate, *A Christmas Carol*, stripped of all the glamour of childhood's associations, seems to me now a deliberate attempt to please the largest possible public by substituting effect for cause, and cosiness for Christianity.

A MEANINGLESS HOLIDAY

And the logical outcome of this, I think, is the joyless, meaningless, and boring orgy of boozing and overeating in which the majority of our countrymen indulge wearily nowadays between December 24 and December 27.

The long-overdue revolt is now beginning, if you recall a letter to a London morning paper recently advocating the abolition of the "nauseating sentimentality" of the Christmas festival from our national calendar and the substitution, for the non-Christian British majority, of a "Day of the Fir Tree" on the Red Hungarian plan.

Undoubtedly the clash was bound to come some time, being one of the inevitable results of a glorious Reformation. But I fear my beloved Dickens, the incomparable magician, the champion of so much good and the enemy of so much evil, unwittingly hastened the anarchy of Luther.

Had Dickens left the Feast alone, "Christmas" might not now be a majority-synonym for "hangover." I think it would have remained for some time as harmless and unprovocative a yearly recurrence in the Stock Exchange calendar as Easter, which as yet bothers hardly anybody progressive, barring a few big business reformers.

So yet another offensive is upon us, it seems, and God bless us all, as Tiny Tim observed. How much more practical if he had added St. Anthony of Padua's cheerful remark that "it is the Fish that survive the Deluge."

CHAPTER 4

Biblical Allusions in *A Christmas Carol*

READINGS ON
A CHRISTMAS CAROL

A Christmas Carol and the Conversion of the Jews

Jane Vogel

Jane Vogel interprets *A Christmas Carol* as an allegory about the conversion of the Jews. In Vogel's analysis, Tiny Tim mirrors Christ and also Timothy, the disciple of St. Paul. Scrooge points to the name of the stone—Ebenezer—set by Samuel to commemorate a Hebrew victory. Scrooge's resistance to Christmas, too, has roots in Hebrew history, namely Israel's rejection of its Messiah and enmity toward Christmas. When the Christmas spirit infuses Scrooge's heart, Scrooge rejects his Hebrew past and is born again. Vogel is the author of *Allegory in Dickens,* from which the following critical analysis is excerpted.

Come Christmas, and Dickensian allegory wears a holiday face wreathed in smiles like a holly-and-berry door knocker, a veritable Scrooge's nephew of a face aglow with brisk walking out of doors (man ever the *homo viator* of City pavements) and with the incurable hope of converting an avuncular world of 'Bah! Humbug!' to 'A merry Christmas, God save you!' Dickens, it seems, will settle for nothing less than the conversion of the Jews—and Christians too.

A Christmas Carol too imparts its holiest Christian message in allegory. Tiny Tim, we know, points to Christ; no secret here. As Bob Cratchit his father tells his wife: 'He told me, coming home, that he hoped the people saw him in the church because he was a cripple and it might be pleasant to them to remember upon Christmas Day who made lame beggars walk, and blind men see.' The child is a divine transparency: 'Spirit of Tiny Tim, thy childish essence was

Excerpted from *Allegory in Dickens,* by Jane Vogel. Copyright © 1977 by The University of Alabama Press. Reprinted with permission from The University of Alabama Press.

from God!' It only remains, then, to recognize Tim as a spiritual sprite or sprig of Timothy, the youthful disciple of St. Paul, the frail and unwell follower whom Paul calls his child and son in Christ. (*1 Tim.* 1:2) Thus seen into, Tiny Tim is like the shining star set atop the Christmas tree last of all amid a universal chorus of 'Ah!'

If Tiny Tim points to Christ, Jacob Marley and Ebenezer Scrooge point to Hebrew time and values past. Wandering in chains for eternity, Marley's wan ghost laments a selfish earthly life in which he never raised his eyes to (in his words) 'that blessed Star which led the Wise Men to a poor abode.' *Jacob*, Israel, rejected Christ and does so still. To see him, picturing what he was in life, or see Scrooge in his dismal room staring at fireplace tiles that depict motifs of ancient Judaeo-Christian history, scenes of Cain and Abel, Pharoah's daughter, Belshazzar, and Aaron's rod, etc., is to grasp the deep-dyed Hebrew components of their souls. To be 'Christians' in such wise, Dickens shows, is in effect to be Jews. Indeed, *Ebenezer* is the name of the stone set by Samuel, Judge of Israel, to commemorate a Hebrew victory over foes. Ebenezer means: 'Hitherto hath the Lord helped us' (*1 Sam.* 7:12) Ebenezer is a stone, and stony-hearted Ebenezer Scrooge lives up to his name.

Thus in allegory the question is no longer only, Will Scrooge, coming to honor Christmas, save a crippled child, but: Will an Ebenezer turn in time FROM Ebenezer or B.C. spiritual ways of vindictive triumph over foes and misanthropic, embattled separatism ('. . . hath the Lord helped US') reminiscent of Israel's pride in exclusive election and disdain for gentiles, TO the ways of Christ mirrored in 'Tiny Tim,' the child poor in spirit and of lowly origin, the 'Tiny' or fragile Christian enterprise debuting then as now and evermore in a cold world. In Scrooge's fanatical resistance to Christmas (Marley, who now sees all, resists no more) is symbolized Israel's blind refusal of its awaited Messiah, and entrenched, age-old enmity towards Christmas. It is all over with Scrooge's seven-years' dead partner, Marley (sad, ironic *seven.*) But in this hopeful seventh anniversary time, will Scrooge finally turn from his and the Hebrew past and, in the spirit of sabbath and seven, looking up at last, see the Star?

Yes! Divine opportunity knocks thrice. Three Spirits guide Scrooge on a journey through time; one misguided earth-traveller is granted a privileged vision of the whole, *sub specie aeternitatis.* Changed wholly by what he sees, the worldling's 'wicked old screw' Screw-*Scroo*-ge *thy neighbor* policy blown clean away (as if one *could* hold fast to the things of this world!), Scrooge awakens on Christmas morning—wakes as for the very first time, born again. The holy Ghosts are with him yet. 'The Spirits of all Three shall strive within me,' he vows. *Three-me:* he rhymes, suddenly all rhymes.

Scrooge's Transformation

Wild with all happiness, frisky as a new-born colt (or soul), Scrooge scrambles madly out of bed this Christmas Day in the morning as from the grave of a long buried life, or waiting death, Marley's inconsolable ghost its symbol, of his soul. Rushing over, he flings wide the sash. The window open: another coffin-casement sprung wide. Ah! Never before such 'golden sunlight; Heavenly sky; sweet fresh air; merry bells. Oh, glorious! Glorious!' Ring out, wild bells! And Heaven and Nature sing. In such descent of radiance from above and rising up in exultation to behold it is previewed the hoped-for resurrection of man to Glory. Scrooge's irrepressible, endless capers, chortles, exclaimings may well recall a child's boundless delight in opening colorfully-wrapped gifts on Christmas morn, which, figuratively speaking, is just what is happening here. How surpassing good to be born again, *and,* of all happy coincidences, born a child 'at Christmas, when its mighty Founder was a child himself.'

Why *such* thanksgiving? Because, the long transfigured night of vision past, it dawns on Scrooge that golden sunlight below ('Oh, glorious!') prefigures ('Glorious!') Glory; that, hark, the whole caroling Creation—sun, air, sky, bells—like the lark at Heaven's gate sings. In Joe Gargery's words, What larks! This is surely no common joy, but tidings of comfort and joy born of revelation of the Joy of joys, Jesu, joy of man's desiring. Of remembering Christ our Saviour was born on Christmas Day. The Eternal bursts in, finally revealed as the wondrous secret of all. The glory of the Lord *shall* be revealed! A 'Heavenly sky,' capital 'H' lofty, intentful, prefigures, promises—Heaven. In such dazzling sunrise, Sonrise; on earth as it is in Heaven. One gust of truly 'fresh air' blows a masking earthly usage from common sights, words, world. In short, Scrooge miraculously reborn intuits the world as allegory, a running figure of the life to come.

How clever the boy is whom he dispatches for the Cratchit turkey (a child ever the angel messenger in Dickens) Scrooge wont, can't, can not, *never can or will* get over. This is because suddenly the whole intelligent, intelligible, intellectually thrilling order the Creator built into Nature and world dawns upon his waking soul. Good Morrow! Dizzy and all but helpless with the wonder of it all, Scrooge grasps the simple secret of Christmas and the uncommon meaning of its dear, common sights. Once, Christmas for Scrooge was a time of feeling imposed upon, of a holiday for his clerk and alms for the poor extorted by foes. Now the reborn Scrooge knows it as a time when the soul of man in outpouring of gratitude inexpressible for the gift of a Saviour must give, and unrelieved of its burden of thanks, give still more. Never enough! In, as Dickens calls it elsewhere, 'the great forgiving Christmas time,' dare we imagine Scrooge dares hope himself forgiven.

The old, crabbed, sunderland 'B.C.' self is no more. The self that stood on the Law, dismissing two gentlemen come seeking Christmas donations for the poor with: 'Are there no prisons? And the Union workhouses?'; that in Hebrew fashion upheld the lawful charity, which in Dickens, is synonymous with service only in the letter, not the spirit of heavenly charity. Now, though, Scrooge realizes that Christmas marks the birth of a spirit of compassion and spiritual largeness not to be so confined. Coming to care tenderly for a crippled child, undertaking to relieve a humble family's sore poverty and to raise its hopes, Scrooge at last enters into full harmony with a Season in which, in Dickens's words, 'we celebrate the birth of that divine and blessed Teacher, who took the highest knowledge into the humblest places, and whose great system comprehended all mankind.' Note, not a Chosen Few, but '*all* mankind,' which sublime ideal shines no less bright in Tiny Tim's message to the world, one so familiar, it may be, we have ceased to see or grasp it any more: 'God bless Us, *Every One!*' (Italics mine.)

DICKENSIAN ALLEGORY

In every nook and cranny of this magic time allegory gleams. Consider Scrooge's spectacular, prolonged fit of chuckling: 'The chuckle with which he said this, and the chuckle with which he paid for the Turkey, and the chuckle

. . . and the chuckle . . . only to be exceeded by the chuckle . . . and chuckled till he cried.' Echoing still the joyous strain, never before such *ch*uckling, *C*ratchit-cherishing, and *c*abs to *C*amden town for the lad (Scrooge insists) upon a Christmas Day. In flurries of snowy 'c,' 'ch,' and 'C,' Christ particles loosed and scattering all over Creation, the boy is off like a shot after the gift intended for secret giving, the gift which, as in allegory itself, the giver remains invisible, the most selfless and so surely the best, truest Christmas gift of all. 'Chirrup, Ebenezer!', words which in Scrooge's youth signaled an end to business and the start of Christmas, the Season to be jolly, are heard again. 'Chirrup': *Cheer up*, merry gentlemen, let nothing you dismay! All is as it was. In one little child found in a poor abode, in Tiny Tims evermore, behold the emblem of the Christ child. 'O, come let us adore Him;' carols the *Carol.*

It is interesting, in the light of the above, to discover a 'Tim-child' motif in a work of four years earlier, *Nicholas Nickleby.* In it, an employee of the Cheeryble Brothers, Tim Linkinwater, a kindly, grey-haired eternal child of the Mr. Dick (*Copperfield*) sort who is 'younger every birthday than he was the year before,' is sympathetically drawn to an ailing young boy. In *Nickleby* the 'Tim' child dies; in the *Carol,* thanks to an influx of spirit in a human heart, it lives. Two 'Tim' figures pointing to the needy child, two appeals for a rebirth of charity, two glimpses of what it means to become as a little child and enter the Kingdom, suggest that a NT-inspired 'Tim' symbolic cluster, *Timothy* a young disciple of St. Paul's, was lodged in Dickens's emblematic imagination and predated its embodiment in the two works. And a Tim-*Ch*eeryble link is likewise Christful to the soul.

The yoke of Dickensian allegory is easy and its burden light. Tiny Tim, recall, hopes it is 'pleasant' for people in church to see him, a cripple, and so be led to remember Christ's kindness to the halt and blind. Note: in Dickens the living symbol more than the preached sermon strikes the Christian lesson warm to the heart.

Old and New Testament Worlds in *A Christmas Carol*

Paul Davis

In his reading of *A Christmas Carol,* Paul Davis examines biblical allusions and the novel's characters. Within this framework, Davis identifies the *Carol*'s division into Old and New Testament worlds, with Marley and Scrooge representing the Old Testament and the Cratchits pointing to the New Testament. Jacob Marley, for example, mirrors a latter-day Jacob while Tiny Tim conjures images of the Christ child. Paul Davis is the author of *The Lives and Times of Ebenezer Scrooge,* from which the following critical analysis is excerpted.

Victorian readers were struck by the reality of the Cratchit family. The *Gentleman's Magazine,* in its original review of the book, for example, praised the "truth" of Bob and Tim: "Tiny Tim is quite perfection, and will serve as an illustration of the great affection shewn by the poorer classes to a diseased or deformed child. Indeed it is impossible to visit the gardens of Hampton Court on a Monday in summer without seeing numerous proofs of this. Often have we watched a mechanic carrying in his arms, a little cripple, eying it with affection, and occasionally pointing out some object of interest to it. Sometimes, he will gently seat it on the grass, watching it while it plucks a daisy, or crawls over the verdant turf. Nor is this to be wondered at. The children of the poor are partakers with their parents of the same dish, the same room, and frequently the same bed. They are the sharers of their poverty as well as of their more smiling hours, and are their constant companions, the objects of their love, whether in weal or woe; and to the credit of the poor, it may be added, that when sickness or old age arrive, the tie of affection is unbroken, and they continue to share in the hard earnings of their offspring." But by the 1870s the portrayal of the Cratchits was much more than simply accurate and sympathetic reportage. In Dickens' latter-day Christmas story, the Cratchits became the Holy Family and Scrooge a nineteenth-century worldly wiseman making his pilgrimage to the humble house of the "poor man's child."

This later Victorian reading of the *Carol* might be described as typological. As an account of the Cratchit family, the story was both contemporary and a re-enactment of the original Christmas story. Although it embodies eternal truths, it does not articulate them as theological abstractions. It is not allegory and it cannot be read as a one-for-one translation of its biblical model. Rather, it embodies the crucial elements of its original. The relation of Scrooge to Tiny Tim in this latter-day scripture is that of type and antitype in traditional typology. As the solitary child abandoned by his father, the psychologically crippled Scrooge is a type to the literally crippled Tiny Tim, his antitype. Carrying his crutch, Tim re-enacts the Christ child, born to carry his cross. To gain an eternal perspective on his life, Scrooge must recognize, however subliminally, the links between himself and Tiny Tim, that he is both "father" and "double" to the child and that they both re-enact their biblical ancestry.

TYPE AND ANTITYPE

Underpinning this typological structure is a division into Old and New Testament worlds, into type and antitype. Linked by the sign on his office to "dead-as-a-doornail" *Jacob* Marley, *Ebenezer* Scrooge inhabits an Old Testament consciousness. He worships golden idols—the specific reason for which his fiancée leaves him—and he grounds his beliefs in the law, in the efficacy of "prisons and workhouses." Just as the biblical Jacob learned God's truths in a dream, so this latter-day Jacob announces a dream to Scrooge that will transform him from a man who legalistically confines his business "to the narrow limits of [his] money-changing hole" to a man who does his "Father's business" (Luke 2:49). The good tidings that Marley's dream brings to Scrooge teach him that "Mankind [is his] business," and "raise [his eyes] to that blessed star which led the Wise Men to a poor abode," leading him to the humble hearth of the Victorian Christ child.

In the Cratchit home, the names—Peter, Martha, Timothy—
tend to be drawn from the New rather than the Old Testament. Tim even links himself with the Christ child when he
hopes "that the people who saw him in the church, because
he was a cripple, . . . might . . . remember, upon Christmas day, who made lame beggars walk and blind men see."
His family name and the crutch (cross) he carries emblem-
ize his role as the antitype "mankind" announced in Jacob's
dream.

Two key biblical allusions support the underlying typological structure of the story. In the opening stave, as Scrooge
sits in front of his fireplace before the arrival of Marley, he
sees the biblical figures decorating the tiles on the fireplace
displaced by the "face of Marley, seven years dead, [that]
came like the ancient Prophet's rod and swallowed up the
whole." The allusion is to Aaron's rod in Exodus 7:12, which
represented divine power in the hands of Moses and Aaron.
The force of this allusion is not merely to suggest that
Scrooge is either an unbelieving pharaoh or a latter-day Is-
raelite who has forgotten his ties to the Lord. The allusion is
typological. Its fulfilling antitype appears in the fourth stave.
When Scrooge, directed by the ominous figure of Christmas
Future, cowers before a corpse stretched out on a bier before
him and is unable to pull back the veil that covers the body,
the narrator comments: "Oh cold, cold, rigid, dreadful
Death, set up thine altar here, and dress it with such terrors
as thou hast at thy command: for this is thy dominion! But of
the loved, revered, and honored head, thou canst not turn
one hair to thy dread purposes, or make one feature odious.
It is not that the hand is heavy and will fall down when released; it is not that the heart and pulse are still; but that the
hand was open, generous, and true; the heart brave, warm,
and tender; and the pulse a man's. Strike, Shadow, strike!
And see his good deeds springing from the wound, to sow
the world with life immortal!"

The allusion is again to Exodus, now to the rod of Moses
striking the rock of Horeb to produce a spring for the thirst-
ing Israelites (Exod. 17:6). This episode, a very common Victorian type, interpreted the "rock of ages" as Christ and the
"cleft" as Christ's wounds flowing with healing blood. In the
typology of the *Carol*, Jacob's dream swallows up the whole
of Scrooge's life and heralds the healing power of the poor
man's crippled child. Dead Marley as type prepares the way

for Tim as antitype, and Tim's wound prompts the conver-
son of Scrooge to good deeds. Scrooge is linked with both
type and antitype, with both Marley and Tiny Tim. He is converted when he gives up being "dead as a doornail" with
Marley and becomes as a little child with Tim. In the vision
of Christmas Future, Peter Cratchit's apt funeral text for his
brother is Mark 9:36, "And he took a child, and set him in the
midst of them." And through this vision Scrooge becomes
"as a child" again. Imitating Marley and Tim, Scrooge becomes an imitation of Christ. He is the body beneath the veil,
whose wounds will flow as good deeds and "sow the world
with life immortal."

SCROOGE'S CONVERSION

Dickens' typological Christmas story links Old and New Tes-
taments in the transformation of Scrooge. It also links the
nativity with the crucifixion and resurrection. Dickens often
associated Christmas and Easter. He described Christmas as
a ceremony of remembering those who had died in the preceding year and celebrated Christ's birth as the annuncia-
tion of His redeeming death and resurrection. The cycle of
the three spirits imitates the cycle of the three days from
Christ's death to His resurrection. As in "A Christmas Tree,"
the holiday in the *Carol* calls up not just the story of Christ's
birth, but the story of his whole life.

For Ruskin and Mrs. Oliphant, and for many later readers
who consider Scrooge's conversion merely an economic or
humanitarian change, the "theological" underpinning of the
Carol has not been apparent. The story's retelling of the
original Christmas story is too displaced, its supernaturalism too natural, to make it seem more than a gospel of food
and drink. But as typology the *Carol* does not distinguish
spiritual truth from its historical embodiment; it also does
not separate the spiritual from the secular. It is not allegorical, abstract, or otherworldly. Unlike the "Scrooge" of the
etherialized *Christmas Eve with the Spirits,* whose death is
the beatific vision of his spirituality, Scrooge's saintliness is
worldly. The wound of his redemption will flow with good
deeds, with active concern for Bob and his family, and he
will achieve a kind of immortal life within this life, an immortality of charity.

As Scrooge leaves his house on Christmas morning and
goes into the streets of the city, London is transformed into

the Celestial City, his kingdom of God on earth. Scrooge does not have to wade through the river of death like Bunyan's Christian to reach the heavenly city. He brings that city to earth. From his wounds flow the good deeds that transform this world and turn the cold and icy streets of London into the golden sunshine of Christmas morning. "He dressed himself 'all in his best,' and at last got out into the streets. The people were by this time pouring forth, as he had seen them with the Ghost of Christmas Present; and walking with his hands behind him, Scrooge regarded every one with a delighted smile. He looked so irresistibly pleasant, in a word, that three or four good-humoured fellows said, 'Good morning, sir! A merry Christmas to you!' And Scrooge said often afterward that, of all the blithe sounds he had ever heard, those were the blithest in his ears."

The Three Magi in *A Christmas Carol*

Donald Perkins

Donald Perkins reads *A Christmas Carol* as an allegory on the soul's resurrection. Perkins argues that Marley's appearance heralds Scrooge's awakening from spiritual death, while the Spirits of Christmas point to the Three Wise Men of St. Matthew's Gospel: Melchior, as the Spirit of Christmas Past, infuses Scrooge's soul with thinking, or memory; Balthazar, the Spirit of Christmas Present, brings the gift of feeling, or awakening of consciousness; Caspar, the Spirit of Christmas Yet to Come, imparts will, or destiny. Perkins is the author of *Charles Dickens: A New Perspective,* from which the following critical analysis is excerpted.

The *Carol* is a Christmas myth, a myth of the Holy Nights, that period of the year between Christmas Eve and January 6, Epiphany. It is a very special period when the highest heaven approaches the earth; when all nature begins to move into activity; when human beings are changed and their true selves become manifest, whether they know it or not, whether they believe it or not. They have experiences which are hardly possible at any other time of the year. It is a 'magic' time and the *Carol* is full of this magic. *Who was Marley?*

Dickens tells us.

> Scrooge never painted out Old Marley's name. There it stood, years afterwards, above the warehouse door: Scrooge and Marley. The firm was known as Scrooge and Marley. Sometimes people new to the business called Scrooge Scrooge, and sometimes Marley, but he answered to both names. It was all the same to him.

Later Dickens tells us that Scrooge 'lived in chambers which had once belonged to his deceased partner'. *Marley was none other than Scrooge himself.* SCROOGE WAS DEAD! We are told that people avoided him. Even the dogs moved away when they saw him coming, which is the behaviour of dogs in the presence of a corpse. Had Scrooge been an evil man, had he been like Fagin, for example, the dogs would have snarled and, perhaps, attacked. The dead man they avoided.

After Scrooge had taken 'his melancholy dinner in his usual melancholy tavern', he made his way to his chambers situated 'in a lowering pile of building up a yard, where it had little business to be'. The house had lost itself, Dickens tells us, when it was a young house, playing hide and seek with the other houses. Like Scrooge who had lost himself between youth and old age.

PRELUDE TO RESURRECTION

As Scrooge inserted his key into the lock of his door his attention was caught by the knocker. He had seen the knocker, night and morning, for as long as he had lived in the house, but without noticing it. A knocker is used to rouse the inmates of a house, to call them to alertness, to summon them to consciousness. Indeed, it may be regarded as a symbol of consciousness. As Scrooge looked at the knocker, it was 'not a knocker, but Marley's face'. In this way Dickens makes it clear that the appearance of Marley, or the ability of Scrooge, under the influence of the magic of Christmas Eve, to come face to face with himself, was the prelude to his recovery of consciousness, which hitherto had been extinguished; and in the centre of this consciousness stood Ebenezer Scrooge, the 'I' of Ebenezer Scrooge! It was the rising of his soul from death into life.

The entrance of 'Marley' into the room where Scrooge was sitting with his gruel, was heralded by a bell.

> It swung so softly in the outset that it scarcely made a sound; but soon it rang out loudly, and so did every bell in the house.

A bell is also a symbol of consciousness, but more penetrating, more demanding than a knocker. Scrooge is fully alert when Marley enters and stands before him. He recognizes himself:

> The same face: the very same. Marley in his pigtail, usual waistcoat, tights and boots; the tassels on the latter bristling, like his pigtail, and his coat-skirts, and the hair upon his head. The chain he drew was clasped around his middle. It was long and wound about him like a tail; and it was made

(for Scrooge observed it closely) of cash-boxes, keys, pad-locks, ledgers, deeds, and heavy purses wrought in steel. His body was transparent; so that Scrooge, observing him, and looking through his waistcoat, could see the two buttons on his coat behind.

That Marley was none other than Scrooge himself is what Dickens wished to convey.

'You are fettered,' said Scrooge, trembling, 'Tell me why?'

'I wear the chain I forged in life,' replied the Ghost. 'I made it link by link, and yard by yard . . . Oh, captive, bound, and double-ironed . . . not to know the ages of incessant labour, by immortal creatures, for this earth must pass into eternity before the good of which it is susceptible is all developed.'

The appearance of Marley, heralded by the knocker and the bell sounding within the 'house', the physical body of Scrooge, marked the arising of consciousness of Scrooge himself as a human being, of the world about him, and of his fellows with whom he lived. He also became conscious of the reality of the spiritual world. We have that incident at the conclusion of Marley's appearance when Scrooge is led to the window and looks out:

The air filled with phantoms, wandering hither and thither in restless haste and moaning as they went. Every one of them wore chains like Marley's Ghost; some few (they might be guilty governments) were linked together; none were free; Many had been personally known to Scrooge in their lives. . . .

Whether these creatures faded into mist, or mist enshrouded them, he could not tell. But they and their spirit voices faded together; and the night became as it had been when he walked home.

We need not think of Scrooge as a unique case or as a figment of the imagination conjured up for the sake of a good story. The *Carol* expressed Dickens's hope for all mankind. In the words of Edgar Johnson: 'What is not so widely understood is that the *Carol* was also consistently and deliberately created as a critical blast against the very rationale of industrialism and its assumptions about the organizing principles of society. It was an attack upon both the economic behaviour of the nineteenth century busi-ness man and the supporting theory of doctrinaire utilitarianism.

Scrooge was the representative business man, even as Bob Cratchit was the representative working man. To neglect Bob Cratchit, to allow him to remain a victim of selfish employers is to create a situation in which none can feel secure. What is needed is not a new system, but a new soul. Dickens, ever concerned for the handicapped, introduces the crippled son of Bob Cratchit, Tiny Tim, the representative of all the children in the age of Dickens who were in need of special care. They, also, must become the concern of the new soul.

THREE SPIRITS

Consciousness having arisen within the soul of Scrooge, he is prepared to receive 'the three Spirits of Christmas' promised by Marley.

> 'How it is that I appear before you in a shape that you can see, I may not tell. I have sat invisible beside you many and many a day.'

> It was not an agreeable idea. Scrooge shivered, and wiped the perspiration from his brow.

> 'That is no light part of my penance,' pursued the Ghost. 'I am here tonight to warn you, that you have yet a chance and hope of escaping my fate. A chance and hope of my procuring, Ebenezer.'

> . . .

> 'You will be haunted,' resumed the Ghost, 'by Three Spirits . . . Without their visits . . . you cannot hope to shun the path I tread. Expect the first tomorrow, when the bell tolls One.'

Who were the Spirits of Christmas who now appear to Scrooge? Dickens answers this question in his own way, for he puts into the mouth of Marley, Scrooge's 'other self', now awakening, the following words:

> 'Why did I walk through crowds of fellow-beings with my eyes turned down, and never raise them to that blessed Star which led the Wise Men to a poor abode! Were there no poor homes to which its light would have conducted *me?*'

The three Spirits of Christmas were none other than the three Wise Men, the three Magi or the three Kings, as they are sometimes called, of St Matthew's Gospel. They are generally named Melchior, Balthazar and Caspar. These three Wise Men, or Kings, may be regarded as representing the threefold being of the soul. The soul of Scrooge, having become conscious, alive, now becomes active in its threefoldness; in its *thinking, feeling* and *willing*.

MELCHIOR

The Spirit of Christmas Past is Melchior who represents 'thinking'. It was Melchior who led Scrooge back into his past so that he remembered what he had long since forgotten and was able to benefit from the wisdom of his remembering. Dickens describes this Spirit.

> It wore a tunic of the purest white; and around its waist was bound a lustrous belt, the sheen of which was beautiful . . . from the crown of its head there sprung a bright, clear jet of light . . . which was doubtless the occasion of its using, in its duller moments, a great extinguisher for a cap, which it now held under its arm.

Memory is not always a comfortable thing. It is easier to forget, and there are those who take measures to assure forgetfulness. *Yet memory is the first great principle of our humanity.* From memory flow *conscience* and *destiny*.

> Perhaps Scrooge could not have told anybody why, if anybody could have asked him; but he had a special desire to see the Spirit in his cap, and begged him to be covered.
>
> 'What!' exclaimed the Ghost, 'would you soon put out, with worldly hands, the light I give? Is it not enough that you are one of those whose passions made this cap, and force me through whole trains of years to wear it low upon my brow!'

The Spirit's light was that of consciousness, from which memory arises. It was necessary that Scrooge should accompany the Spirit of Christmas Past. It was necessary that he should remember. [As Karl König stated in a lecture in 1967:]

> Man has not only consciousness; he has also *memory* . . . but memory is only possible where consciousness is: without consciousness memory could not come about. Within the sphere of consciousness, memory can unfold—yet they are by no means the same. Consciousness gives us a certain awareness of all that is around us . . . but with consciousness alone we would never know anything. Every second, every part of a second, just consciousness would be present; nothing would connect the flow of time, the coming and going of experiences, the difference of what we see, hear, smell, taste, do and so on. There memory sets in. The power of memory is the ability to re-create. The power of memory is that something which has once happened is not lost: it can be remembered, rebuilt, re-created—in many different forms.

So the Spirit of Christmas Past, whom we have recognized as Melchior, conducts Scrooge back into his past, and

Scrooge remembers. He is able, with the help of the Spirit, to re-create the scenes of his boyhood and young manhood, and relive them. He is able to think again into his past, clearly and truly. He sees himself as the lonely boy at school; as an apprentice enjoying the Christmas party given by his master, Fezziwig; as the young man in love with a dowerless girl, but in love with money more. It is a painful experience for Scrooge which in the end becomes too much for him.

'Remove me!' Scrooge exclaimed, 'I cannot bear it!'

He tried to extinguish the Spirit's light and succeeded in doing so; but the reader is not disturbed for he perceives the light shining with ever-increasing brightness from Scrooge's own head. His thinking is alive again. He has received the gift of Melchior.

BALTHAZAR

When Scrooge awoke he was 'prepared for almost anything, he was not by any means prepared for nothing; and, consequently, when the Bell struck One, and no shape appeared, he was taken with a violent fit of trembling'. As he lay in bed he was 'the very core and centre of a blaze of ruddy light', which streamed from the adjoining room. He decided to investigate and as his hand was on the lock 'a strange voice called him by his name, and bade him enter.' He obeyed. The Spirit of Christmas Present was there in an easy estate upon a couch.

> There sat a jolly Giant, glorious to see; who bore a glowing torch, in shape not unlike Plenty's horn, and held it up, high up, to shed its light on Scrooge, as he came peeping round the door.
>
> 'Come in!' exclaimed the Ghost. 'Come in! and know me better, man!'
>
> . . .
>
> 'I am the Ghost of Christmas Present,' said the Spirit. 'Look upon me!'
>
> Scrooge reverently did so. The Ghost was clothed in one simple green robe, or mantle, bordered with white fur.

Apart from the general 'heartiness' of the situation in which the Ghost of Christmas Present appears, Dickens clearly indicates who he is.

> This garment hung so loosely on the figure, that its capacious breast was bare, as if disdaining to be warded or concealed by any artifice.

Dickens refers to this 'bare breast' later as though by way of emphasis, and also writes of the 'kind, generous, hearty nature' of the Spirit, and 'his sympathy with all poor men'. Here in the figure of the Spirit of Christmas present, we have *Balthazar*. Under his ministry the *feeling* of the soul of Scrooge is awakened. In the company of Balthazar Scrooge visits the home of Bob Cratchit and the house of his nephew. He is able to experience the love and joy which emanates from both places.

> 'Spirit,' said Scrooge, with an interest he had never felt before, 'tell me if Tiny Tim will live.'
>
> 'I see a vacant seat,' replied the Ghost, 'in the poor chimney corner, and a crutch without an owner, carefully preserved. If these shadows remain unaltered by the Future, the child will die.'
>
> 'No, no,' said Scrooge, 'Oh, no, kind Spirit! say he will be spared.'

So we reach the climax of this episode. Scrooge sees something strange protruding from the skirts of the Ghost.

> 'Forgive me if I am not justified in what I ask,' said Scrooge, looking intently at the Spirit's robe, 'but I see something strange, and not belonging to yourself, protruding from your skirts. Is it a foot or a claw?'
>
> 'It might be a claw, for the flesh there is upon it,' was the Spirit's sorrowful reply. 'Look here.'
>
> From the foldings of its robe, it brought two children; wretched, abject, frightful, hideous, miserable. They knelt down at his feet, and clung upon the outside of his garment.
>
> 'Oh, Man! look here. Look, look, down here!' exclaimed the Ghost.
>
> They were a boy and a girl. Yellow, meagre, ragged, scowling, wolfish; but prostrate, too, in their humility. Where graceful youth should have filled their features out, and touched them with its freshest tints, a stale and shrivelled hand, like that of age, had pinched, and twisted them, and pulled them into shreds. Where angels might have sat enthroned, devils lurked; and glared out menacing. No change, no degradation, no perversion of humanity, in any grade, through all the mysteries of wonderful creation, has monsters half so horrible and dread.
>
> Scrooge started back, appalled . . .
>
> 'Spirit! are they yours?' Scrooge could say no more.

'They are Man's,' said the Spirit, looking down upon them.
. . .

'Have they no refuge or resource?' cried Scrooge.

'Are there no prisons?' said the Spirit, turning on him for the last time with his own words. 'Are there no workhouses?'

The bell struck twelve.

Dickens used both laughter and tears in his service of the soul. The consequence of his efforts to arouse consciousness was not only the arising of memory, but the awakening of *conscience!* We may *think* about situations and about other human beings, and this leads to memory, the first great principle of humanity. When we begin to *feel* for other human beings, to sympathize, that is to suffer with them and for them; when the heart, no longer cramped, begins to move *outwards* into the world, then *conscience,* the second great principle of our humanity, awakens. It awakens, as in the case of Scrooge, in the midst of tears and in the company of shame, but the soul cannot be said to be truly alive, in the feeling realm, until conscience is active. There arises in the soul a feeling of responsibility, conscientious responsibility, for one's fellow men. This feeling may also be extended to Nature, but that is not the concern of Dickens in this story. Conscience belongs to the feeling realm. There can be no true activity of conscience apart from love. It is, of course, related to memory, the first principle, as our experience will reveal.

Scrooge 'had left undone the things he ought to have done' as a human being and the results of his neglect were the death of Tiny Tim and of the two children who appeared beneath the cloak of the Spirit. As his experience under the guidance of the Spirit of Christmas Present, his heart became sensitive and out of the sensitive, feeling heart, conscience appeared. This was the gift of Balthazar.

CASPAR

The Spirit of Christmas Yet To Come we have identified as Caspar who, according to legend, was a black man, an African, the representative of the darkened will. His advent into our story is described by Dickens in the following words:

The Phantom slowly, gravely, silently approached. When it came near him, Scrooge bent down upon his knee; for in the very air through which this Spirit moved it seemed to scatter gloom and mystery.

It was shrouded in a deep black garment, which concealed its head, its face, its form, and left nothing of it visible save one outstretched hand. But for this it would have been difficult to detach its figure from the night, and separate it from the darkness by which it was surrounded.

He felt that it was tall and stately when it came beside him, and that its mysterious presence filled him with a solemn dread. He knew no more, for the Spirit neither spoke nor moved.

'I am in the presence of the Ghost of Christmas Yet To Come?' said Scrooge.

The Spirit answered not, but pointed onward with his hand.

'You are about to show me shadows of the things that have not happened, but will happen in the time before us,' Scrooge pursued. 'Is that so, Spirit?'

We are impressed by the contrast with the other two Spirits, especially with the Spirit of Christmas Present. For the first time Dickens uses the word 'phantom' to describe this Spirit. 'The phantom,' he writes, 'slowly, gravely, silently approached.' This may be only an alternative word used for the sake of variety, but I feel sure it was suggested to Dickens by his conception of the Spirit. It was 'phantom-like' in a sense in which the other two Spirits were not. The head, face and form were invisible. Only its outstretched *hand* could be seen by Scrooge. It was difficult for him to detach its figure from the night or to separate it from the darkness; and it does not speak in spite of Scrooge's efforts to persuade it to do so. So we have invisibility and silence. As the bright clear jet of light from the head of the Spirit of Christmas Past indicated thinking, and the bare breast of the Spirit of Christmas Present indicated feeling, so the description of the figure of Christmas Yet to Come phantom-like, enveloped in a mystic darkness, silent before all questioning, indicates the will.

Under the guidance of this Spirit Scrooge plunged into spiritual darkness. There is no light here, there is no humour. The account which Dickens gives of Scrooge's experiences in the company of this Spirit is almost harrowing. It is like the final stage of an initiation. But Scrooge does not retreat. His deep desire is to press on into the future even though that future be dark and full of pain.

'Lead on!' said Scrooge. 'Lead on! The night is waning fast, and it is precious time to me, I know. Lead on, Spirit!'

We notice that his whole attitude has changed since his thinking, revealing *memory,* and his feeling, revealing *conscience,* were enlivened. Now, through the activity of the will, *destiny* appears before him. This is the true gift of Caspar. *The third great principle of our humanity.*

Scrooge is guided by the Spirit into the city where he hears some of his business associates discussing his death. He sees himself upon his death bed, unmourned, alone, except for some strangers who are only interested in what they might steal from his corpse. He visits the home of Bob Cratchit where Tiny Tim lies dead. Finally he enters a churchyard where he looks upon his own grave and reads his name upon the tombstone.

> A churchyard. Here, then, the wretched man whose name he had now to learn, lay underneath the ground. It was a worthy place. [Dickens cannot resist the use of irony in the description of such a place.] Walled in by houses; overrun by grass and weeds, the growth of vegetation's death, not life: choked up with too much burying; fat with repleted appetite. A worthy place!
>
> . . .
>
> 'Before I draw nearer to the stone to which you point,' said Scrooge, 'answer me one question. Are these the shadows of the things that Will be, or are they the shadows of things that May be, only?'
>
> . . .
>
> 'Men's courses will foreshadow certain ends, to which, if persevered in, they must lead,' said Scrooge. 'But if the course be departed from, the ends will change. Say it is thus with what you show me!'
>
> The Spirit was as immovable as ever.
>
> Scrooge crept towards it, trembling as he went; and following the finger, read upon the stone of the neglected grave his own name, EBENEZER SCROOGE.
>
> 'Am *I* the man who lay upon that bed?' he cried upon his knees.
>
> The finger pointed from the grave to him, and back again.
>
> 'No, Spirit! Oh, no, no!'

So Scrooge sees himself as he had been—a *dead* man.

In this scene the whole meaning of destiny is gathered into a few sentences. For Scrooge, as he had been, with his dead soul, this is the inevitable end. It is the picture, harrowing indeed, of the destiny of the man with the dead soul. Death appears as finality, lonely, painful, terrible. Yet, as the

Carol makes clear, this death is not necessarily final. There can be a rebirth. There is the power of the Resurrection.

> 'Spirit!' he cried, tight clutching at its robe, 'hear me! I am not the man I was. I will not be the man I must have been but for this intercourse. Why show me this, if I am past all hope!'
>
> For the first time the hand appeared to shake.
>
> 'Good Spirit,' he pursued, as down upon the ground he fell before it: 'Your nature intercedes for me, and pities me. Assure me that I yet may change these shadows you have shown me, by an altered life!'

Within the destiny of all of us lies the death of the physical body. We cannot avoid it. With understanding we can be grateful. This death can be beautiful, the entering of the soul into the light of its spiritual home. But if the soul dies! This was the concern of Dickens, as it must be for us.

We possess our future; it is, so to speak, in our hands, at our feet. We make of it what we *will.* It belongs to the realm of the will, but it is influenced by our thinking and feeling, or by our memory and conscience. Scrooge is the representative of those men who had the power to change the conditions in which many of their fellow human beings lived—and died, 'being born expressly to do it,' as Dickens says: men who become insensitive to the needs of others. In the *Carol* Dickens shows how the dead soul can be born again through the revival of memory and the awakening of conscience, leading to the path of its true destiny. Dickens lifts the veil and we see, standing before us, *man,* in all his strength and weakness, in all his light and darkness; with his infinite possibilities; *man* who, by the power of 'the Christmas magic' can conquer death and free himself from his prison.

RESURRECTED SOUL

In the last stave, 'The End of It', Dickens leaves no doubt in the reader's mind that Scrooge is a new man, a true man. He is full of abundant life which he can hardly control! It is important to note that Dickens is able to use his humour again. Having passed through the darkness with Scrooge the reader is able to laugh with him. He is able to open his heart and to receive the 'new man' with gladness. There is one sentence which is full of significance, but which could easily be overlooked. In the excitement caused by his newly discovered self Scrooge remarks:

'I don't know how long I've been among the Spirits. I don't know anything. I'm quite a baby. Never mind. I don't care. I'd rather be a baby.'

Who is this baby whom Scrooge now experiences? Compared with the other members of our being, our 'I', or ego, is a baby. It is a baby lying in the arms of the soul; the Christmas picture. Now that the soul of Scrooge has become alive the ego can be nursed and nourished. The ego begins to move, to become active, to call attention to its presence. Looking back upon the story we can feel that the three Spirits, the three Kings, the three Magi, came to the ego, the true self, of Scrooge, before whom they knelt in homage and presented their gifts. Thinking, feeling and willing acknowledge the greater king.

Dickens makes it clear, at the beginning of the story, that Scrooge avoided his fellow human beings, as they avoided him. This, of course, was inevitable. His soul being dead, mummified and insensitive, there was no possibility of contact through the medium of sympathy, interest or concern. Scrooge was visited by his nephew who invited him to dinner on Christmas day. The nephew's talk about Christmas angered Scrooge.

'Don't be angry, uncle. Come! Dine with us tomorrow.'

Scrooge said he would see him—yes, indeed he did. He went the whole length of the expression, and said he would see him in that extremity first.

But now:

In the afternoon he turned his steps towards his nephew's house.

He passed the door a dozen times, before he had the courage to go up and knock. But he made a dash, and did it!

'Is your master at home, my dear?' said Scrooge to the girl. Nice girl! Very.

'Yes, sir.'

'Where is he, my love?' said Scrooge.

'He's in the dining-room, sir, along with the mistress. I'll show you upstairs, if you please.'

'Thank'ee. He knows me,' said Scrooge, with his hand already on the dining-room lock. 'I'll go in here, my dear.'

He turned it gently, and sidled his face in, round the door. . . .

'Fred!' said Scrooge.

. . .

'Why bless my soul!' cried Fred, 'who's that?'

'It's I. Your uncle Scrooge. I have come to dinner. Will you let me in, Fred?'

Will you let me in, Fred? Scrooge is now able to seek his place in the human community, and is heartily welcomed. And this is really the end of it, an end which was, at the same time a new beginning, although we should note as Dickens would have wished, that the wages of Bob Cratchit were raised and Tiny Tim did not die.

As Humphry House wrote in his comment on the *Carol:* Dickens 'was not a Benthamite or Philosophical Radical or Chartist or Owenite or Christian Socialist or Young Englander, nor did he start a Dickens Party. But he did . . . attempt to sketch a kind of human being which might become a focus of reformist sentiment. If everybody were like this, he seemed to say, the complex evils of the world would automatically be cured, the nostrums unnecessary.' Do we believe this? Dickens speaks to us over one hundred and forty years, through one hundred and forty Christmas festivals. As we read his story we can feel the breath of the Spirit in this time 'when the air is thin' in 'the prison of this lower world'. We are encouraged and we are grateful that the *Carol* still lives amongst us. In any case we all agree that the prayer of Tiny Tim, with which our story closes, is needed not only at Christmas-time, but through all the year:

GOD BLESS US EVERY ONE!

Chronology

1812

Charles Dickens born February 7, to John and Elizabeth Dickens; War of 1812 begins with United States.

1814

John Dickens transferred to London.

1817

John Dickens transferred to Chatham.

1821

Charles Dickens starts school.

1822

John Dickens transferred to London.

1824

John Dickens arrested for debt and sent to Marshalsea Prison; Charles Dickens begins work at Warren's Blacking Factory.

1824–1826

Attends Wellington House Academy in London.

1827

Works as law clerk; improves his education at the British Museum Reading Room.

1830

Meets Maria Beadnell.

1831

Becomes reporter for the *Mirror of Parliament.*

1832

Becomes staff writer for the *True Sun.*

1833

First published piece appears in the *Monthly Magazine;* slavery abolished in British Empire.

1834

Becomes staff writer on the *Morning Chronicle;* street sketches published in the *Evening Chronicle;* meets Catherine Hogarth.

1836

Sketches by Boz published in book form; marries Catherine Hogarth; plays *The Strange Gentleman* and *The Village Coquettes* produced at St. James's Theater; meets John Forster, a lifelong friend and biographer; Ralph Waldo Emerson publishes *Nature.*

1836–1837

Pickwick Papers published in monthly installments.

1837

Pickwick Papers published in book form; begins installments of *Oliver Twist* in *Bentley's Miscellany;* play *Is She Your Wife?* produced at St. James's Theater; first child, Charles, born; Catherine's sister Mary Hogarth dies suddenly; Victoria becomes queen of England; Thomas Carlyle publishes *The French Revolution.*

1838

Nicholas Nickleby appears in installments; *Oliver Twist* published in book form; first daughter, Mary, born; first railroad train enters London.

1839

Nicholas Nickleby published in book form; second daughter, Kate, born; People's Charter, stating six demands for voting and representation for the poor; Chinese-British Opium Wars begin; end 1860.

1840

Dickens edits *Master Humphrey's Clock,* a weekly; *The Old Curiosity Shop* appears in installments and in book form; England annexes New Zealand; Queen Victoria marries Prince Albert; James Fenimore Cooper publishes *The Pathfinder.*

1841

Barnaby Rudge appears in *Master Humphrey's Clock* and in book form; Dickens's second son, Walter, born; the magazine *Punch* founded; Ralph Waldo Emerson publishes *Essays.*

1842

Dickens tours America with Catherine; *American Notes* published; Alfred, Lord Tennyson publishes *Poems;* anesthesia first used in surgery.

1843

Martin Chuzzlewit appears in monthly installments; "A Christmas Carol" published for Christmas; William Wordsworth becomes poet laureate.

1844

Dickens tours Italy and Switzerland; *Martin Chuzzlewit* published in book form; "The Chimes" published for Christmas; Dickens's third son, Francis, born; first message by Morse's telegraph.

1845

Dickens produces the play *Every Man in His Humour;* "The Cricket on the Hearth" published for Christmas; Dickens's fourth son, Alfred, born; Edgar Allan Poe publishes *The Raven and Other Poems.*

1846

Dickens creates and edits the *Daily News; Dombey and Son* appears in monthly installments; *Pictures from Italy* published in book form; "The Battle of Life: A Love Story" published for Christmas; Irish potato famine results in mass emigration to United States; repeal of Corn Laws, which regulated grain trade and restricted imports; Elias Howe invents sewing machine.

1847

Dickens starts a theatrical company and takes *Every Man in His Humour* on a benefit tour; Dickens's fifth son, Sydney, born; Charlotte Brontë publishes *Jane Eyre;* Emily Brontë publishes *Wuthering Heights;* Henry Wadsworth Longfellow publishes *Evangeline.*

1848

Theatrical company performs for Queen Victoria; theatrical company performs *The Merry Wives of Windsor* to raise money for preservation of Shakespeare's birthplace; *Dombey and Son* published in book form; "The Haunted Man" published for Christmas; Dickens's sister Fanny dies.

1849

David Copperfield appears in monthly installments; Dickens's sixth son, Henry, born; Henry David Thoreau publishes "Civil Disobedience."

1850

David Copperfield published in book form; Dickens establishes and edits *Household Words;* Dickens's third daughter, Dora Annie, born, dies in infancy; Elizabeth Barrett Browning publishes *Sonnets from the Portuguese;* Tennyson becomes poet laureate; Nathaniel Hawthorne publishes *The Scarlet Letter.*

1851

Dickens and theatrical company perform charity plays; Dickens's father, John, dies; Nathaniel Hawthorne publishes *The House of the Seven Gables;* Herman Melville publishes *Moby-Dick.*

1852

Bleak House appears in monthly installments; *A Child's History of England* published in book form; Dickens's seventh son, Edward, born; Harriet Beecher Stowe publishes *Uncle Tom's Cabin.*

1853

Bleak House published in book form; Dickens gives first public reading from the Christmas books; travels to France and Italy.

1854

Hard Times appears in installments in *Household Words; Hard Times* published in book form; Henry David Thoreau publishes *Walden;* Crimean War begins; ends 1856.

1855

Little Dorrit appears in monthly installments; Dickens and family travel to Paris; Walt Whitman publishes *Leaves of Grass.*

1856

Dickens purchases Gad's Hill.

1857

Little Dorrit published in book form; Dickens spends year on theatrical productions.

1858

Dickens separates from Catherine; Dickens gives public readings; Henry Wadsworth Longfellow publishes *The Courtship of Miles Standish.*

1859

Dickens ends *Household Words;* begins *All the Year Round; A Tale of Two Cities* appears in *All the Year Round* and in book form.

1860

Great Expectations appears in weekly installments.

1861

Great Expectations published in book form; *The Uncommercial Traveller*, a collection, published; George Eliot publishes *Silas Marner;* U.S. Civil War begins; ends 1865.

1862

Dickens gives many public readings; travels to Paris; Victor Hugo publishes *Les Misérables;* Lincoln issues Emancipation Proclamation, freeing slaves.

1863

Dickens gives public readings in London and Paris; mother, Elizabeth, dies; Lincoln delivers Gettysburg Address.

1864

Our Mutual Friend appears in monthly installments.

1865

Dickens suffers a stroke, leaving him lame; *Our Mutual Friend* published in book form; *The Uncommercial Traveller*, a second collection, published; Lewis Carroll publishes *Alice in Wonderland;* Leo Tolstoy publishes *War and Peace;* rapid postwar industrialization in United States.

1866

Dickens gives public readings in Scotland and Ireland; Fyodor Dostoyevsky publishes *Crime and Punishment.*

1867

Dickens travels to America to give public readings; England grants dominion status for Canada.

1868

Dickens gives public readings in England; Louisa May Alcott publishes *Little Women.*

1869

Dickens begins *The Mystery of Edwin Drood;* Mark Twain publishes *Innocents Abroad;* imprisonment for debt abolished; Suez Canal opened.

1870

Dickens gives farewell public reading in London; *The Mystery of Edwin Drood* appears in monthly installments; becomes seriously ill, June 8; dies, June 9; buried in Poet's Corner, Westminster Abbey, June 14.

FOR FURTHER RESEARCH

ABOUT CHARLES DICKENS AND *A CHRISTMAS CAROL*

Peter Ackroyd, *Dickens.* New York: HarperCollins Publishers, 1990.

John Butt, "Dickens's Christmas Books," in *Pope, Dickens, and Others.* Edinburgh: Edinburgh University Press, 1969.

G.K. Chesterton, *Charles Dickens: The Last of the Great Men.* New York: The Readers Club, 1942.

Philip Collins, ed., *Dickens: Interviews and Recollections.* London: Macmillan Press, 1981.

Earle Davis, *The Flint and the Flame: The Artistry of Charles Dickens.* Columbia: The University of Missouri Press, 1963.

Fred Kaplan, *Dickens: A Biography.* New York: William Morrow, 1988.

Stephen Leacock, *Charles Dickens: His Life and Work.* London: Peter Davies, 1933.

Jack Lindsey, *Charles Dickens: A Biographical and Critical Study.* New York: Philosophical Library, 1950.

John Lucas, *The Melancholy Man: A Study of Dickens's Novels.* New York: Barnes and Noble, 1970.

Harlan S. Nelson, *Charles Dickens.* Boston: Twayne, 1981.

J.B. Priestley, *Charles Dickens and His World.* New York: Charles Scribner's Sons, 1961.

Stephen Wall, ed., *Charles Dickens: A Critical Anthology.* Harmondsworth, England: Penguin, 1970.

Angus Wilson, *The World of Charles Dickens.* London: Martin Secker & Warburg, 1970.

Edmund Wilson, "Dickens: The Two Scrooges," in *The Wound and the Bow.* Boston: Houghton Mifflin, 1941.

WORKS BY THE AUTHOR

Charles Dickens, *A Christmas Carol.* With an introduction by Walter Allen. New York: Harper and Row, 1965.

————, *A Christmas Carol.* With an introduction by G.K. Chesterton. London: Waverley Book Co., 1915.

————, *A Christmas Carol.* With an introduction by Edgar Johnson. New York: Columbia University Press, 1956.

————, *A Christmas Carol.* With an introduction by A.R. Tomkins. London: Blackie and Son, 1966.

————, *A Christmas Carol and Other Haunting Tales.* New York: Doubleday, 1998.

————, *A Christmas Carol: The Public Reading Version.* New York: The New York Public Library, 1971.

————, *The Letters of Charles Dickens.* New York: Oxford University Press, 1965.

ABOUT DICKENS'S TIMES

Jerome H. Buckley, ed., *The Worlds of Victorian Fiction.* Cambridge, MA: Harvard University Press, 1975.

Amy Cruse, *The Victorians and Their Reading.* Boston: Houghton Mifflin, 1935.

John W. Derry, *A Short History of Nineteenth-Century England.* London: Blandford Press, 1963.

Walter E. Houghton, *The Victorian Frame of Mind.* New Haven, CT: Yale University Press, 1966.

R.J. White, *The Horizon Concise History of England.* New York: American Heritage, 1971.

ORGANIZATION TO CONTACT

Dickens Society (DS)
Department of Humanities and Arts
Worcester Polytechnic Institute
Worcester, MA 01609-2280

Phone: (508) 831-5572
Fax: (508) 831-5878

The society conducts and supports research and general interest in the life, times, and works of Dickens. Its scholarly journal, the *Dickens Quarterly,* includes an annual index and bibliographies.

INDEX

powerful effect, 53, 54
as shown by magical qualities
in plot, 48
shown in title and
headings, 47
and storybook atmosphere, 52
humor in, 61
and tears, 157
irony in, 41, 86
paternalism of, 57, 62–63
Switzerland, 24

Tale of Two Cities, A, 28, 131
Tatler (newspaper), 14
Tennyson, Alfred Lord, 73, 75
Ternan, Ellen, 25, 28
Thackeray, William, 11, 18,
24, 111
themes, 90
biblical, 73, 74, 128, 146, 148
and Book of Job, 72
and Exodus, 147
Catholicism, 23, 135–36, 137
connectedness of society, 50
domestic ideal, 116, 117–18
and family as model for
society, 119
inspired by childhood, 15
and issues contemporary to
Dickens's time, 43
marriage, 98–99
metaphysical innocence, 70–71,
73, 79
and childhood, 80–81
immutability of, 71–72
loss of, 74, 76
and materialism as attempt
to recover, 75–76, 77
Scrooge's rediscovery of,
81–82
redemption of Scrooge by
Christmas, 137
resurrection, 159–61

social criticism, 19, 28, 56, 114
and attack on utilitarianism,
83, 84–88, 152
on employer/employee
relations, 118
on need to care for
handicapped children, 153
spiritual, 160
superficiality of, 137–38
time, 39–41, 79, 107, 108
including historical time,
43–44
including time after death,
42–43
see also allegory; Christmas;
characters, Ebenezer Scrooge
Theocritus, 124
Thomas, Deborah, 58–59
Trollope, Anthony, 38
True Sun (newspaper), 15
Turn of the Screw, 39

Ulysses (Joyce), 76

*Varieties of Religious Experience,
The* (James), 88
Victoria, queen of England, 25
Victorian Age in Literature, The
(Chesterton), 137
Vogel, Jane, 140

War and Peace (Tolstoy), 80
Waters, Catherine, 111
Weller, Mary, 13
Wellington House Academy, 15
Westminster Abbey, 29
Wilson, Angus, 20, 28–29
Wilson, Edmund, 68
Wordsworth, William, 73, 80
World of Charles Dickens, The
(Wilson), 20
Wyndham, D.B., 135

12/03 ∅

11/05   1   7/05

5/06 ②
    5/16 ③ 1/14